A LILLIPUT MAGAZINE ANTHOLOGY

1937-46

The Best Writing From Its First Ten Years

Chris Harte

Sports History Publishing

Stefan Lorant
Editor 1937-40

Tom Hopkinson
Editor 1940-46

Sydney Jacobson
Assistant Editor 1937-48

Kaye Webb
Assistant Editor 1940-47

Charles Fenby
Associate Editor 1940-44

Alison Blair
Assistant Editor 1936-39

Sports History Publishing

First published in 2024

ISBN : 978-1-898010-19-7

Editor : Susan Lewis

Consultant Editor : John Aaron McMaster

Series Editor : Rupert Cavendish

Layout & Design : Nick Beck

Contact : rupertcavendish47@gmail.com

Printed and bound in Wales

Sports History Publishing titles are distributed by

Dodman Books
Morston Barn
Binham Lane
Morston
Norfolk NR25 7AA

Recent Books by the Author include

Lilliput Magazine: A History & Bibliography
C.B.Fry's Magazine: A History & Bibliography
Fores Sporting Notes & Sketches: A History & Bibliography
Strange Stories of Sport
The Badminton Magazine: A History & Bibliography
The Captain Magazine: A History & Bibliography
The Sporting Mirror: A History & Bibliography
Hunting in Carmarthenshire 1741-1975
A History & Bibliography of Baily's Magazine of Sports
Old Gold: Carmarthen Town Football Club
Watching Brief: A Journalists' Odyssey
Rugby Clubs and Grounds
English Rugby Clubs
Britain's Rugby Grounds
Reminiscences of a Sportswriter
Sports Books in Britain

In Preparation

A History and Bibliography
of Men Only Magazine
(to be published in 2026)

STORY INDEX

THE CREATION OF LILLIPUT

Istvan Reich was born in Budapest in February 1901 and following the death of his father sixteen years later he changed the family name to Lorant. In 1923 he became known as Stefan Lorant, a name he was known by for the rest of his life.

During his somewhat undistinguished academic school life Lorant excelled as a violin player, playing solo at one time with the leading Hungarian baritone Imre Pallo. His personal life, however, was complicated. He married four times and had children within and out of wedlock. His second recognised child (for others were never publicly mentioned) was Virginia who was born in March 1938, the result of a long liaison with Alison Blair, a woman who had, by then, financed *Lilliput* Magazine.

At the age of thirteen Lorant purchased a camera and, in the family bathroom, processed his film. In Budapest the weekly newspaper *Erdekes Usag* boasted of "having secured the patent to reproduce pictures by rotogravure." Lorant sent them his pictures, taken by chance, of Count Gyula Andrassy, a former foreign secretary of the monarchy. These were published in August 1914 and set Lorant on the path of photo-journalism.

He started taking photographs for theatre magazines and had many put in the trade journal *Szinhazi Elet*. When the editor was called up for war service he handed the editorship to a young man who was only five years older than the schoolboy Lorant. The two worked well together, the new editor being Sandor Kellner (later known as Alexander Korda) who went on to become a noted film producer, director and screenwriter. Then, at the end of 1916, the coronation of King Karl provided Lorant with a front cover in the weekly magazine *Das Interessante Blatt*.

In March 1920 he moved to Vienna and soon became a cameraman for the film director Otto Kreisler before going to Berlin to be part of the great period of German silent films. From 1925 to 1928 he edited several German picture magazines, including *Das Magazin* and *Ufa Magazin*, and then secured the plum post as editor of *Muncher Illustierte Presse*. This position allowed him the freedom to display and bring together his visual and intellectual talents in one combined entity. Lorant's skill within the liberal paper saw the circulation rise from around fifty thousand copies for each issue to nearly two million by the end of 1928.

Years later Lorant reflected on his time in Berlin remembering how so many of the writers and photographers who worked for him emigrated and either Anglicised or changed their names. His list contained many who would contribute to the future *Lilliput*.

The fear of the future came about on 31 January 1933 when Hitler was appointed Chancellor of Germany. On 13 March Lorant was arrested and jailed: for six and a half months he languished in prison. He decided to keep a diary to record the truth about his situation during the early days of the regime. He noted down everything he saw on odd scraps of paper, pocket handkerchiefs and the backs of letters and envelopes. The eventual publication of *I Was Hitler's Prisoner* three years later went to numerous print runs.

After the Hungarian Consulate-General had made repeated requests for Lorant's freedom he was released on 25 September and was deported to Budapest. The next day he went to see Miklos Lazar, the publisher of the daily newspaper *Pesti Naplo*. Within two hours he was offered a job as editor of the paper's magazine. He stayed for six months, having by then realised that the most talented movers and shakers had left the country and he wanted to do the same.

Lorant arrived in London on 17 April 1934 having spent time in Paris trying to find a publisher for his manuscript. Eventually Victor Gollancz purchased it for an advance of one-hundred and ten pounds and after signing a contract he went to see an old Hungarian friend Burt Garai, managing director of the Keystone Press Agency. He was immediately given a contract to write articles for circulation.

Soon Odhams Press made contact with him and he was given a short-term contract to try and revive a dying magazine titled *Clarion*. Along with the assistant editor, Tom Hopkinson, they completely changed the tone of the publication and prepared a dummy with the title *Weekly Illustrated*.

Lorant then started to collect material which would shape the first few issues of the new pictorial weekly. For the first issue Odhams printed a large number of the extra-large sized magazine with the words "incorporating *Clarion*" within the logo on the front cover. By its sixth issue it was selling two-hundred thousand copies.

Weekly Illustrated was the first modern popular picture weekly and became the model for all other picture magazines such as *Life* and *Look*. But Lorant only edited the first twenty-two issues. It was him and Hopkinson; no other staff and a complete lack of marketing. There were quarrels over the print runs and even though the Odhams hierarchy tried to persuade him to stay, the non co-operation from management had taken its toll. Added to which Lorant's name never appeared as editor, nor in his contributions within the pages. Even in the trade journal *The Writers and Artists' Yearbook* the name Maurice Cowan was given as editor although Hopkinson, in his autobiography, put it in a different light.

He wrote that Cowan, who had become well established in the company, and Lorant did not get on together. Both kept different working hours which Cowan found difficult to accept. According to Hopkinson, Lorant said: "Tom, I cannot work where I am not appreciated and no one here understands what I am doing." With that Lorant resigned and spent the next two years as a freelance journalist.

Ever the wanderer he found himself in Sanary-sur-Mer, then a fishing village some eleven kilometres west of Toulon on the Cote d'Azur. He was spending the late summer of 1936 with thirty-year-old Alison Blair.

Blair was the daughter of a journalist, Hamish Blair, who had been the editor of the *Calcutta Statesman* newspaper. She was privately educated and had gone on to read English and Psychology at Girton College, Cambridge. She possessed the distinctive upper-class manner and accent of one raised under the Raj.

Although she had written articles for newspapers while in India, Alison Blair found it more difficult and frustrating to break into the British market. She had little success and was getting frustrated. Her marriage was slowly crumbling as her husband, Ian Hooper, spent more time either at work in the City of London or at his club. Their politics also differed with he and his extended family supporting Stanley Baldwin while Blair was a Labour voter and also a member of the local branch of the party.

One Sunday morning in the spring of 1936, Hooper announced casually over breakfast that Lotti Gorn, a female magazine illustrator acquaintance he had invited to lunch, would be bringing a friend with her. One of their guests asked who it was and was told the name was Stefan Lorant to which the reply was: "Oh. He had a letter in the *New Statesman* the other day about the German situation."

Blair's initial impression of Lorant was of something large, foreign, shaggy and outlandish who reminded her of a gipsy violinist. But it was his conversation which made her listen carefully. Lorant warned of a future war, one which Blair had tried to explain to her husband, who now had to listen to the foreboding of a luncheon guest. As she wrote: "He was the first direct contact any of us had had with the new European political realities."

The next time Lorant visited it was at Alison's invitation. Her husband found their discussion boring and left them to talk. The result was that Lorant invited Blair to join him in the South of France for a summer holiday.

She later wrote: "*Lilliput* was born of a chance encounter with exiles based in the South of France at a cafe in Sanary-sur-Mer, a regular daily meeting point for refugee writers such as poet and dramatist Ernst Toller, writer Arnold Zweig and novelist Lion Feuchtwanger, among others. On a table was a copy of an American pocket magazine, *Coronet*. Leafing through it idly, Lorant remarked how easy it should have been, with such resources, to produce something more worthwhile. The only interesting thing is the size. If one only had a little capital."

Blair added: "Feuchtwanger suggested 'You should start something in England.' but Lorant admitted to having no capital. Then I asked him how much would he need. We agreed £2,000 so I told him that I would supply the money as I had received an unexpected windfall to invest for myself and it was this sum which I proposed to use."

Tom Hopkinson, who had stayed with *Weekly Illustrated*, wrote in his autobiography: "After his sudden departure I had lost touch with Stefan. I knew he had had some success with his book and wrote articles for newspapers. I would also hear of him from girls I knew, but whom he had evidently got to know a great deal better than I had. Then, in the early summer of 1937, I came across him again as we were both walking through Covent Garden, picking our way among the squashed fruit and cabbage stalks."

He looked despondent. He frowned: "The editors in this country, they do not like my work. Or if they like it, they do not pay enough. There is only one thing for me to do." I asked him what it was. "I become an editor myself," he replied.

Lorant and Blair started work on what was to become *Lilliput* in the rented apartment of the Hungarian photographer Zoltan Glass situated in Charlbert Court, St.John's Wood, London. They produced a dummy issue in June 1937 and had some printed by the Arthur Press of Bayswater.

It had a striking cover illustration by the artist Walter Trier, whom Lorant knew from Germany, showing an aerial view of the landscape of London with the River Thames running down the middle. On a huge, outstretched hand stands a man reading the magazine. On the cover itself was printed: "10 articles, 10 short stories, 50 photographs, 10 cartoons, 6d." There were one-hundred and thirty pages and no advertising. This numerical precis of the contents already stressed the good value the reader would receive for his money.

Blair recalled: "Stefan's technical knowledge of printing and typography; the experience he had already acquired of English printing firms, made him able to choose with unerring judgment the best one for our purpose and to make advantageous terms. His technical proficiency gave him authority with printers and compositors and served to avoid wasting time and money on attempting the impossible. His knowledge of layout made the most both of material and of the machine."

"Although he was a foreigner in a strange country he knew always where to lay hands on the best author for the particular subject, the right artist or photographer for the illustrations, and the one library for any necessary research. His judgment of ability was unerring whether its possessor's name was known or unknown. And although we could not always at first afford to pay authors adequately they seemed glad to write for *Lilliput* sensing their possibilities in Stefan's hands."

Blair continued: "He drove people hard, never allowing an inaccuracy or imperfection to pass, forcing revisions or a re-write if necessary; yet he was a constructive critic who not only could tear a manuscript to pieces but could also help to put it together again creatively."

Whatever she wrote, Blair was the real strength behind Lorant. She had proposed the name of the magazine and, as Assistant Editor, had made the decisions as to which articles should be considered for publication. Her technical know-how was different to Lorant's and as a team they worked together perfectly.

As Lorant's biographer states: '*Lilliput* was different in size and shape, concept and content, than the other magazines which he had edited. It appealed to a more discrete readership. In bringing new European writers to his pages, he gambled that the readership would share his enthusiasm.'

As with *Weekly Illustrated*, Lorant was anxious to achieve high initial sales. Seventy thousand copies were printed of which fifty-nine thousand were sold. Contrary to the anticipated reduction in sales after the first issue they actually increased: August 61,086; September 69,369; October 72,146; November 71,205, December 77,414 and the January 1938 edition (published on 15 December) sold over eighty-thousand copies.

However, the Audit Bureau of Circulation figures, certified on 12 January 1938, suggested that the *Lilliput* sales were averaging an extra 4,789 copies per issue. Success brought its difficulties; printers wanted to be paid in advance, distributors to pay in arrears. All these problems built up even with the arrival and financial help of Sydney Jacobson who took the title of being another Assistant Editor.

The balance sheet for the magazine's first six months came to £1,280 for each issue while the income was only £960. The loss for the first six months was £1,920 which, in reality, was an incredible achievement particularly considering that to this point it had carried no advertising. For the seventh issue Lorant opened *Lilliput* to a limited number of advertisements. The net advertising revenues came to £325, so just breaking even. Four issues later revenue was £460 and after that it continued to rise.

Sydney Jacobson gambled on putting his gratuity gained from working on the *Statesman* in India into the company, now called Pocket Publications Limited. The rented offices were at Lincoln's Inn Chambers in London's Chancery Lane. All four of them (for Charles Windust had joined in a waged capacity) worked as many hours of the day they could. Blair remembers spending nights by her desk and using a sleeping bag so she could start work early each morning.

Once word got around that Lorant was paying his contributors his former colleague Tom Hopkinson went to see if he could be commissioned to write for the magazine. He was invited to provide a piece to be titled: 'The Summer Term at Oxford.' The article was rejected twice, the second time by Lorant in person with Jacobson adding weight to the decision. Blair who, at the time was pregnant with Lorant's child, was now only part time in the office.

Hopkinson was extremely annoyed and so Lorant agreed to take him to lunch a few days later to discuss the situation. On 12 May 1938, Hopkinson arrived at the office to be met by an excited Lorant who was wearing a new suit and silk shirt. He ran down the stairs, seized Hopkinson's arm and hurried him down the street. When they were well clear of the building he spoke.

"Tom, I am a very rich man! Very rich men lunch only at the Savoy. We go to the Savoy!" Over lunch Lorant revealed that he had sold *Lilliput* to the Hulton Press for £20,000 and that they had also asked him if he would now plan to start a new magazine for the company. Even before lunch was over Lorant had agreed to take Hopkinson on to his new project subject to the approval of Hulton's general manager, Maxwell Raison.

If nothing else, Lorant was a man of honour to those who had supported him. Of the £20,000 the sum of £5,604 went to pay off debts. On her original investment Alison Blair received £5,300 and Jacobson, who had invested £1,500 nine months earlier, received £2,000 bearing in mind he had been receiving a salary while neither Lorant nor Blair drew any form of payment, except for £6 a week for expenses.

The build-up to the sale of *Lilliput* started when Raison had paid a visit to the offices to see if Lorant would assist in a proposed political magazine which Hulton's (through a third-party) were considering creating. Lorant was curious that his visitor did not know more about him particularly as he was also in the publishing business. Raison seemed unaware that Lorant had written an account of his prison experience and had not read any of Lorant's articles in the English newspapers. Until this meeting, he appeared completely unaware of Lorant's experience with German, Hungarian and English pictorial magazines.

Behind Lorant's desk were bound volumes of the *Munchner Illustriete Presse* to which Raison took an interest and asked to borrow a volume. He returned a few days later with the borrowed volume and subsequently arranged for Lorant to meet publisher Edward Hulton. The meeting ended badly but a few days later Raison returned and offered to buy *Lilliput*. An agreement was reached, with all staff remaining and Lorant to create another magazine. This one to be called *Picture Post*.

Under Hulton's able circulation manager, Vernon Holding, *Lilliput*'s circulation continued to climb. By June 1940, the audited circulation was 251,763. With increased advertising revenue, before the year was out, Hulton Press regained its full investment in the magazine.

Sales kept rising through the decade to be 507,770 for the January to June 1947 period. Lorant's midas touch also took *Picture Post* to unforeseen heights. An initial print run of 750,000 for the first issue (705,954 sold) became sales of 1,025,548 two months later and 1,350,000 two months after that. Six months following the first issue, the Hulton Press print order had climbed to some 1.7 million copies.

Life for Lorant was becoming difficult. He was still in a relationship with Alison Blair and in autumn 1938 she gave birth to Lorant's child, a girl they named Virginia. Ian Hooper would not give her the divorce she requested and after discussing the matter with him then decided to take all three of her children to America for safety. Hooper who had been called up by Naval Intelligence and posted to Athens agreed with this move.

Lorant followed not long afterwards, but only for six weeks, before returning in early 1940. He then soon found himself classified as an enemy alien and had his bicycle and car confiscated. He was told by the police he could no longer live at Aldenham House Club near Elstree so he moved to the Savoy Hotel. Although he was annoyed at being made to move the fact was that Aldenham had become a secret establishment as the British Broadcasting Corporation's wartime headquarters for Overseas Broadcasting.

In July 1940, fearing a German invasion and the fact he was named on the Gestapo list of people to be shot immediately when arrested, Lorant sailed from Liverpool in the *SS Britannic*, the last passenger ship to leave England for America. However, some years later it became clearer as to why Lorant had left in such a hurry when an adverse report was attached to his Home Office confidential file. It claimed that he had avoided paying taxation on most of his salary; on the royalties of his best-selling book and on the money for the sale of *Lilliput* to Hultons. In a letter sent from Edward Hulton in early March 1953, Lorant was advised not to return to England.

To quote his biographer, Michael Hallett: "Hell hath no fury like a woman scorned, and so it was with Lorant. The irony, of course, was that this same country, which had served punitive reparations on its enemy, was now playing the same game with its friend. The Nazis had ruined him financially, and the British were hell-bent on doing the same. Lorant believed beyond question that his actions were morally and ethically sustainable. He had earned his money; and he was keeping it."

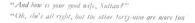
"And how is your good wife, Sultan?"
"Oh, she's all right, but the other forty-nine are more fun"

October 1937

" My God, Frobisher, your mother!"

March 1939

THE FIRST TEN YEARS

The first issue of *Lilliput* hit the newsstands on 15 June 1937 and was an immediate success. It was a pocket-sized, racy, irreverently illustrated and in the new-style paperback format. It appeared two years after the first Penguin paperback and at the same price.

Stefan Lorant was the editor with Alison Blair as his deputy. From the third issue they were joined by Sydney Jacobson and a few months later by Kaye Webb who started in the role of secretary. Charles Windust was taken on to be the office boy and general factotum.

From the beginning, with Lorant wanting to introduce more European culture to an inward looking people, he made three appointments. The first, as Paris Editor, was George Boloni (1873-1951) a Hungarian formerly Gyorgyne and also known as Sandor Kemeri. A writer and poet, Boloni had excellent literary contacts with those of his countrymen who had fled to France.

The Vienna Editor was Count Kurt Strachwitz (1890-1961) who had an office in Universitats Strasse. Here he could easily liaise with the artistic cafe-culture and pass on any writings for Lorant's consideration.

The third European appointment was that of Imre Gal (1901-69) who had changed his surname from Sandor. He was based in a Budapest suburb although his literary activities saw him spending a considerable part of each day in newspaper and magazine offices. He did not last long as Budapest Editor, fleeing to France, then America, as war drew ever closer.

One of the main items of early issues were the photographic juxtapositions. As Lorant explained in his book, *Chamberlain and the Beautiful Llama*: "We wanted the magazine to be original and successful. We worked in two small rooms with no organisation and no great resources. We had to give a lot: stories, articles, cartoons, photographs and reproductions of paintings in full colour."

He added: "Captions were important. People are always more intelligent than publishers and editors believe." He likened two of the juxtapositions, that of the rich, sad, ruthless oil-king John Rockefeller to a happy, old Hungarian peasant woman. Under Rockefeller he wrote 'riches: under the peasant woman 'poverty.' Lorant commented: "I felt sure that readers would understand the point of these. They would connect the two for themselves and what the pictures meant to say."

The front cover design was created by Prague born Walter Trier. It showed a young couple with their little black dog lying on the grass and reading the magazine. In bringing European writers and illustrators to his pages Lorant gambled that his readership would share his enthusiasm. He also started a number of unknown writers on to their career paths.

It was in issue three that Lorant introduced infra-red photography. He had obtained a number of photographs taken by the young French artist

Pierre Boucher. There were five published, all being of night views taken in Morocco in darkness the human eye could not penetrate. Lorant wrote: "By the use of material which gives special ultra-red sensitivity photographs can be made in the dark. With the help of these cameras we can now record what the eye cannot see."

Also in this issue Lorant commented: "The success of the first two numbers of *Lilliput* has exceeded all our hopes. Everywhere it has had a warm welcome and many of our readers have been kind enough to write and tell us of their appreciation and to assure us that we are meeting a long-standing demand in the magazine world. For these congratulations and good wishes we are grateful."

The advent of Sydney Jacobson into the office changed the balance of the editorial team. Blair, who was still in a relationship with Lorant, was not a person given to arguing with her lover. However, she was known for her sharpness and wit, more so for her particular dexterity with the photographic juxtapositions.

Like many magazines the best period of its existence was its first dozen years when it filled the prescription of Lorant's editorial in the March 1939 issue. "Our success," he explained "owed to the need for a low-priced magazine for intelligent readers: one which would mingle humour and information; which would be both funny and thought-provoking with no axe to grind; and which would have the courage to present an undistorted, unbiased picture of our times."

From the start the focus of *Lilliput* was contemporary and international. Although known for its photographs, Lorant introduced to his mainly British readership writers of worldwide reputation. In the first volumes contributors included James Agate, Margot Bennett, Leslie Halward, John Peskett and Victor Pritchett; and the Europeans Ferenc Molnar, Sidonie-Gabrielle Colette, Lajos Biro, Clarisse Meitner, Karel Capek and Odette Keun all of whom brought new writings to the readers.

British and Irish writers providing stories included Liam O'Flaherty, Theodora Benson, Cecil Forester and Maurice Richardson. Light verses came from Stevie Smith and Ogden Nash with celebrated writers of a generally heavier manner, such as Ernest Hemingway, not being excluded.

From the first issue Lorant proved he was able to capitalise on his European experience and contacts, particularly when drawing material from the photographic agencies of continental Europe. But the general tone of *Lilliput* was light with the articles and stories rarely more than a thousand words.

In making appointments Lorant was influenced by the talent he saw in people. Tim Gidal was one of the German cameramen who had fled to Britain and he had done a story using thirty-five millimetre film and was looking for somebody to process it for him. The name of Edith Kaye was mentioned and he telephoned her and made an appointment. Kaye was also

German and she, too, had fled the Nazi regime.

She duly processed the film which Gidal took along to Lorant and asked him what he thought of the pictures. Lorant looked at them closely and said: "Never mind your story, who did your printing for you?" Edith was contacted straight away and immediately hired to run the *Lilliput* and *Picture Post* darkrooms where she remained for the next twenty years

With the magazine's first birthday in sight Alison Blair and the office secretary Marie Norton decided to send out letters to selected individuals to elicit responses of congratulation which could be used in future issues. Replies came back from invited and, in some cases, uninvited people.

From newspaper proprietors Lords Beaverbrook (*Daily Express*) and Rothermere (*Daily Mail*) both commented on "the vigour and originality of the magazine," with *News Chronicle* editor Gerald Barry commenting: "You have set the pace in pocket magazines in this country and your several imitators are the best tribute you could have to your enterprise."

In a review, *The Sunday Express* noted: "A bedside book full of interest for every taste. There are beautiful photographs, articles of humour, comment and information, pictorial reproductions of art masterpieces, cartoons and an interesting series of some of the very first photographs ever taken."

But it was the novelist Naomi Mitchison whose remarks fairly well summed up what Lorant was trying to achieve. She wrote: "When I first found my seven-year-old reading *Lilliput* in bed, I was rather shocked. However, on further consideration it struck me as being thoroughly good for her. Instead of absorbing the usual fairy-dope for middle-class children, she may actually get hold of a few bits of genuine truth about this peculiar world. Long may you keep out of the paws of the various censors, official and unofficial, who keep on, like the great sloth, trying to sit on us."

Hardly two months had passed since the Hulton Press had purchased the magazine when Edward Hulton started to interfere in its running. He and Lorant had differing views about various subjects more so as Hulton was being ear-bashed by his Conservative cronies at the Garrick Club about the anti-German stance being taken while Lorant was at the opposite end of the political spectrum.

Eventually the disagreement boiled down to the *Lilliput* front covers. Hulton noted: "I don't like the magazine's front covers. They do not convey the spirit of the publication, its freshness and vivacity. They are far too simple."

Lorant was blunt in his reply. "That is precisely what I intended. The whole idea behind *Lilliput*'s covers is simplicity. They are thought out in terms of one colour, a different basic colour each month. The young man and young woman and their dog appear every time. They are just ordinary people, like you and me, but unlike us they always do exactly what we would like to do. In summer they bathe in the blue Mediterranean, in spring they ride on the backs of camels in Egypt, and they winter in St.Moritz."

He added: "They never work. They are always happy. And that is the spirit of *Lilliput*, light-hearted and care-free. And so I'll keep to these covers." Hulton was not convinced. "All the same, I don't like them," he replied. In the end they agreed to let the readership decide what they liked and asked for comments.

The letters poured in from all over the world. After just three weeks there were 1,267 votes to keep the front cover and only thirty-five against although these latter ones contained a number of caveats, comments and suggestions. Edward Hulton was magnanimous in defeat and awarded cash prizes to the best three ideas one of whom was, ironically, from a German Baroness.

By now Lorant was firmly in charge of *Lilliput*. Alison Blair hardly visited the office following the birth of her child and Sydney Jacobson was often editor in all but name as Lorant spent time creating dummies of the soon to be launched *Picture Post*. He had the full backing of Edward Hulton to edit both magazines and with Tom Hopkinson now having joined the staff had an able deputy for the new ventures.

Hopkinson's name had been put forward by Lorant and he was interviewed for the position of Assistant Editor in mid-June 1938 by Maxwell Raison the Hulton Press managing director. In his letter of appointment Raison expressed his hope that Hopkinson could start as soon as possible as he was needed.

Soon after the launch of *Picture Post*, Lorant was boasting of its 750,000 initial print run adding: "*Lilliput* had a print run of 215,000 for the October 1938 issue: And I am editor of both." Lorant was, at times, very pre-occupied with letting readers of the magazine know how popular it had become. In March 1939 he wrote on the final advertising page that "... this month's issue is having a print run of 225,000 copies." The following month he wrote "of 235,000 copies," and in June of "275,000 copies of our magazine." However, this increase meant that the Sun Engraving Company did not have the facilities to meet the demand and so the Hulton Group entered into an agreement with printers Hazell, Watson & Viney who had the capacity at their huge printing works in Aylesbury.

Lorant's relationship with Alison Blair became more one-sided as he conducted affairs while she seemed to become more devoted to him. She finally took the decision to go to America in mid-1939 with her three children. She left the offices of *Lilliput* in May, never to return, even though her name would stay in the credits as an Assistant Editor, then Associate Editor, for more than another year.

Although Lorant made sure that exiled European writers were able to contribute to the magazine he also attracted a number of British authors who were titled. Lady Hore, Lord Dunsany, Lord Berners and Baron Kinross had stories published in early 1939 along with a number of wives who used their nom-de-plumes instead of their married titled names.

At the same time Lorant was editing *Picture Post* and was having no compunction in using *Lilliput* articles in the new magazine. He also commissioned pieces from James Laver, Ritchie Calder, John Langdon-Davies, Antonia White and Arthur Cronin of a much larger length than could be used in the pocket-sized publication. He made occasional use of illustrator Nicolas Bentley and used North American stories from Stephen Leacock and James Thurber.

With Lorant away Tom Hopkinson took over the editorial chair and subtle changes were instituted without much notice being taken of them. More space was given to occasional writers while the main burden of office cartoon work fell on the shoulders of the talented Victoria Davidson (then known as either Lilli Commichau or Victoria Victor).

Hopkinson took it upon himself to write an editorial for the November 1939 issue. It read: "This is the first number of *Lilliput* to be prepared in wartime. War is a disaster but, like in all times of stress, it produces great writing. In this issue we publish examples of the war literature of all ages from the earliest Anglo-Saxon battle-song to the narrative of a U-boat commander."

"This war will produce its great writers. Some of them may be at present unknown. We hope that their stories will appear first in *Lilliput* and we offer a prize each month for the best new story of the war published by us. Other war stories accepted will be paid for at our usual rates. Stories should not exceed thirteen hundred words."

The trade journals of the time stated that payment was "three to five guineas per one thousand words," which would have attracted a number of potential new contributors. Hopkinson knew that Sydney Jacobson was shortly to join the army along with assistants Lionel Birch and a future editor, Richard Bennett, so he needed to fill possible gaps in the magazine.

He added in his comments: "*Lilliput* will continue to appear in its present form. We will continue our policy of giving our readers an intelligent and unbiased selection of the work of the world's best writers, artists and photographers, foreign as well as British. We will publish articles on subjects of special importance by leading experts; also cartoons and picture comparisons; and not to lose our sense of humour."

To keep all of these promises Hopkinson needed a special person to take control of the organisation of the office. Little did he then know that a young woman who had just transferred from *Picture Post* to become Sydney Jacobson's secretary, and suddenly showed excellent editorial skills, would fill this important post. Her name was Kaye Webb.

Not long before his trip to America Lorant was faced with a number of problems. With the beginning of the war advertising had collapsed with the late 1939 issues having only eight pages, down from thirty-two in pre-war numbers. This concerned the Hulton organisation so much that the general manager Maxwell Raison questioned as to whether *Lilliput* and *Picture*

Post could continue publishing. After discussion it was agreed to carry on while regularly reviewing the situation.

Lorant's talents were many and varied. By his own force of presence and a will of never giving up he was able to persuade advertisers back to the magazine in such numbers that by Christmas he had forty pages to add to the ninety-six of text, photographs and cartoons.

In his role as Acting Editor, Hopkinson was informed that the price of *Lilliput* had to change so he wrote an editorial for the January 1940 issue titled '*The War Price of Lilliput*.' In it he noted that the cover price "had to be increased from sixpence to sevenpence an issue," and detailed the facts that "paper is up in cost by thirty-five percent; that we are now printing three-hundred thousand copies each issue; that seventy-five tons of paper are used every month; the increase in production costs have risen £600 each number; distribution costs have been raised by thirty percent; insurance has risen sharply; our rent has been increased; we have to still pay the wages of staff away on active service, and other unanticipated and non-budget costs."

Lorant returned at the end of January 1940 for what would be his final six months as editor of both *Lilliput* and *Picture Post*. By the time of his departure Kaye Webb was working on the photographic section of *Lilliput* and in early August was de-facto Assistant Editor although the Hulton organisation did not agree at the time. Not long afterwards Hopkinson was appointed editor and he immediately confirmed Webb as his assistant. She wrote at the time about: "... what incredible chances and challenges that offers me."

She was now the only female writer in the office and along with Hopkinson they nurtured new artistic and literary talent as well as appointing regular contributors.

Knowing that Lorant would not be returning, Hopkinson went about recruiting new staff who could work on both magazines. His first appointment was that of Charles Fenby who was the founding editor of the *Oxford Mail*. He wrote later: "It was with great difficulty that I managed to persuade my old friend to leave the *Mail* after his twelve years in the hot seat. He did eventually join us to be in charge of the writing side. It was a fortunate choice, since with him Charles brought a more thorough journalistic background than I had ever managed to acquire, plus a wide range of acquaintances in various fields of life whom we could call on for articles or advice."

Fenby, who had been at Oxford with Hopkinson, had started on the editorial staff of the *Westminster Gazette* and then the *Daily News*. Their first problem was to resolve the situation regarding photographers as both Hans Baumann and Kurt Hubschmann had been carried off for internment to the Isle of Man. Then other staff writers were called up for army service, which, with other conscriptions, reduced the staff from thirteen to five.

Hopkinson had appointed Honor Balfour when Lorant was away on his first visit to America. She also studied at Oxford University and was a journalist on the *Oxford Mail* who would stay with the Hulton Press for six years. Then came Macdonald Hastings, a writer familiar with country life and sport, who was soon followed by Maurice Edelman who stayed for five years before becoming a Member of Parliament.

Albert Lloyd had been a script writer for both the drama and features departments of the *BBC*, but in 1940 they considered him far too left-wing to be allowed to handle programmes 'during a war for democracy' and he was asked to leave. Hopkinson employed him at once and he stayed for eleven years before returning to broadcasting. The last of the intake was Anne Scott-James who had begun her career with *Vogue* in 1934. She started as a writer and in 1941 was made the first Women's Editor of both magazines.

In his autobiography Hopkinson relates of that time: "In addition to the journalists recruited onto the staff, and to my great excitement, we found a remarkable new photographer. Bert Hardy was a young cockney and when he came to see me he was already an experienced cameraman. To try him out I offered him a difficult assignment. The Blitz had started and I asked him to take pictures inside street shelters. No flash must be used and the pictures must make the reader feel he was inside with the shelters in semi-darkness while bombs were falling. Bert passed the test triumphantly; I at once took him on the staff and he was soon a mainstay of both magazines."

As the war started to become closer to home, and more men were being called up for military service, many of the regular writers and illustrators were not able contribute to the magazine. Although the quality of the stories in late-1940 were still of a good calibre, the illustrations started to decline in standard. The cutting captions were replaced by more comical views while the drawing of certain cartoons lacked substance. Some illustrators only appeared once; others infrequently.

However, *Lilliput* quickly became a favourite with the Forces, partly because of its size and relatively undemanding text but equally because of its good humour and occasional nudes. With Tom Hopkinson now confirmed as Editor of both *Lilliput* and *Picture Post*, and having Kaye Webb as a genuine deputy, he was able to write: "*Lilliput* was an easy magazine to sell. It did not attack or criticise. It simply made one laugh and because of this sales soared into the hundreds of thousands."

By early 1942, Webb wrote in her unpublished memoirs: "The war has really put a rocket under my career." She mused: "*Lilliput's* popularity has enabled me to ring up anyone I like and to invite them to contribute." She approached all the literary luminaries of the day, including George Bernard Shaw, Ernest Hemingway, Cecil Forester, Osbert Sitwell, John Betjeman, Herbert Wells and Max Beerbohm.

"Everyone wanted to appear in *Lilliput*," Webb wrote. "*Punch* still did not use by-lines and writers would always rather have a shop window. We liked our cartoonists recognisable; we liked to be able to say, "That's a Langdon" or "That's a Searle." Franta Belsky was another new cartoonist; Gerard Hoffnung sent in drawings from Highgate School." Kaye admitted that she did not like the schoolboy's efforts, "but Tom insisted he had genius, which indeed he had, so we kept on using him."

Ideas poured into the office and Webb noted how they tended to come in waves. "We have had twenty cartoons of a BBC announcer sitting in front of a microphone wearing a sou'wester while he says 'And here is a gale warning' or some variation on the idea." She added: "It happened with stories too; one month a load of tales about a talking horse, or a singing dog; another month a spate of mysterious train journeys that don't stop at the usual station but roll on into ghostly country."

Later in 1942, Kaye Webb received her civilian call-up papers and was scheduled to be designated to work in a munitions factory. She handed her papers to the Hulton hierarchy who then replied for her stating: "Kathleen Webb is Assistant Editor of *Lilliput* and she also assists with editorial work for *Picture Post*, the staffs of the two papers having been merged since the war. She is the only person remaining on our staff who has had long contact with *Lilliput* and who is able to deal with the photographs and with the handling of the magazine for press. In present circumstances she is indispensable to *Lilliput* and we wish to make the strongest possible claim for retaining her services. There would be practically no possibility of replacing her in present conditions." Nothing more was heard of the matter.

Webb was correct in her view that *Lilliput* attracted all sorts of groups. In the early days Lorant had used many of his European photojournalist contacts to supply pictures which he could use. The list seemed endless with many eventually fleeing from Europe to start again in either Britain or, mainly, America.

Looking back, the quality of these people is quite breath-taking: Bill Brandt, Pierre Boucher, Henri Cartier-Bresson; Gertie Deutsch, Tim Gidal, Zoltan Glass, Gyula Halasz, Philippe Halsman, Vaclav Jiru, Camilla Koffler, Jean Moral, Paul Popper, Man Ray, Wolfgang Suschitzsky and the greatest Russian spy of the 1930s in Edith Tudor-Hart: all of whom brought a completely new dimension to photography in the staid British magazines of the time.

Lorant had hit home with his photographic juxtapositions and in many ways they made *Lilliput*, even to the extent of being quoted in a House of Commons debate. The bubble burst when Lorant fled to America and the decision on photos to be used fell on to the shoulders of Macdonald Hastings. He did not have the wherewithal or contacts and very quickly the punchy European style was replaced by bland British efforts.

Agency contributions were largely used over the following months as with the war raging there was little else available. It would be some time before the standard rose above mediocre and even then the quality of the images never again reached the heights known under Lorant's editorship.

By the summer of 1942, Hopkinson was becoming in awe of his prized photojournalist Bill Brandt, so much so that he wrote of him in a preface to a series of images. He reflected: "Some time in the spring of 1936 a young man came into the office where I was working. He carried, under his arm, a book of photographs which showed more sharply than I had seen before, how a human eye and a piece of mechanism can combine, not so much to record the world as to impose a particular vision of the world upon it."

"This slim young man could take photographs. He had an eye for social contrasts and on top of this he had an acceptance of the world for what it is. He worked for some weeks on *Weekly Illustrated* where I then was and I learned rather more about him. Having been born in Germany; lived in Switzerland and then moved to Paris, he had been strongly influenced by the photographers Eugene Atget and Man Ray. Also by the artists Pablo Picasso and Georges Braque, and by Luis Bunuel and other directors of the new surrealist films."

"It was under these Paris influences that Brandt developed what is the outstanding quality of his work: its sense of mystery. In all the best of his pictures there is a sense of immanence, of something about to happen. These are rare gifts with which to start any kind of work. He has a delicate sense of irony and humour. As he went out of the door, having been commissioned by *Lilliput* to photograph 'London in the Moonlight,' Kaye Webb, the assistant editor, remarked: 'And remember, we don't want a lot of whacking great moons floating about all the pictures.' Brandt gave one of his vague, courteous smiles, and vanished."

Frustration took hold of Hopkinson, as shown in a memo he wrote to Edward Hulton. He said: 'This is to explain the sort of difficulties we are up against in trying to secure pictures dealing with the war for use in *Lilliput* and *Picture Post*. These difficulties are of two kinds.'

'First, the difficulty of getting matters arranged. One example will do. We wrote three times to the Admiralty; once before the war; once at the outbreak; once more recently, asking permission to take pictures chiefly of an Admiralty board meeting.'

'No letter was even acknowledged, and weeks later the pictures we had asked permission to take appeared in the *Daily Sketch* and elsewhere. They had received permission and we had to buy the pictures and use them ten days later.'

'Secondly, and this is our real trouble, both *Lilliput* and *Picture Post* are fairly new publications and both work along new lines. Many people like them but very few have any idea as to how they achieve their effects. These are twofold: telling a story in pictures and by always having natural pictures, never posed ones.'

'The idea of telling a story in pictures is still something new in Fleet

Street. Few papers attempt to do it and only about half-a-dozen cameramen in the whole country understand the technique.' Hopkinson then went on to explain how newspaper photographers took their pictures and how his team wait until the subject is doing their normal duty and then his cameraman gets to work.

With staff still being conscripted at regular intervals, the non-commissioned contributions from readers proved to be a life-saver. The one person who grew in stature during this time was Kaye Webb. She wrote: "Contributors wandered into the office in Shoe Lane. Stevie Smith brought in her poems while Victor Pritchett was nice enough to allow me to reshape one of his articles because it wasn't what Tom wanted. John Pudney would come in and talk about ideas. It was an agreeable time."

Webb was in the centre of a vibrant, talented coterie of poets, writers and artists who flourished in the hedonistic wartime atmosphere of blacked-out Soho and Fitzrovia. She took the sculptor Henry Moore to lunch; sent Bill Brandt to photograph Laurie Lee; invited Dylan Thomas to write picture captions and in turn got introduced to the poet and artist Mervyn Peake.

By the Spring of 1943, *Lilliput* had run out of steam. Kaye Webb reflected at the time: "The magazine drags along without much joy. Tom is really rather difficult to work for. He has appointed a new man [John Symonds] whose function is to improve the literary standard of the paper. He is to share my room!"

Hopkinson, on the other hand, was much more optimistic. "For me," he wrote," the one or two afternoons each month which I spent working on the magazine were made easy and enjoyable because all the real work had already been done by the assistant editor Kaye Webb and her helper Mechthild Nawiasky. Webb was a lively and attractive girl so that writers, artists and photographers were constantly coming into the office to talk to her and going away finding they had promised to do a couple of drawings or write a funny article by the day after tomorrow."

The list of noted contributors had been endless due to Webb's easy manner. She discovered Bill Naughton who, at the time, was a lorry driver. She remembered: "He came wandering into the office with a badly typed story; it was the first one he ever got published."

In later years Hopkinson admitted that *Lilliput* had been oddly staffed for a popular magazine. "Neither Kaye nor Mechthild had received any regular journalistic training. I had been recommended to use John Symonds and when I interviewed him I asked what his experience had been on newspapers and magazines. He answered engagingly that he had almost none. Later I learned that he had been researching for his father's books."

"This seemed to me such an unusual introduction to working on a magazine that I suggested he join us for three months on a minimum salary till we saw how useful such self-training might prove. At the end of this period we were glad to keep him."

Whatever the contents were the magazine was still popular among all classes of people. The troops went for the photographs and illustrations while others found interest in the artistic sections.

With the war taking a turn in mid-1944, Kaye Webb did not seem to have a care in the world. Her second husband had been posted overseas and so she took every opportunity to enjoy herself. Whether or not she meant to approve them but certain published stories were rather *risque* with one, in the August 1944 issue, presumably slipping past the censor. The author was Maurice Edelman who, the following year, would start a lengthy term as a Member of Parliament.

They had met when he had visited the *Lilliput* offices and it was he who arranged her first broadcast when she interviewed him about a book of his which had recently been published by Penguin. In later years Webb admitted: "He was very attractive to women." She added: "He also taught me how not to split my infinitives and for about three years we were truly great friends. I really adored him." Together they wrote an adaptation of an Alfred de Musset play which was offered to the Arts Theatre, without success. Then Edelman left for North Africa as a war correspondent and they only ever met once again.

By now Webb was taking on more magazine responsibility, writing occasional articles and the monthly Lemuel Gulliver column as Mac Hastings had become a war correspondent. She was industrious and ambitious, broadcasting book reviews for the *BBC Home Service*; telling American radio stations about life in London and having a column in the forces publication *Gen*.

Tom Hopkinson, having divorced the neurotic novelist Antonia White, had married the photojournalist Gerti Deutsch. In November 1944 he and his family moved from the safety of the countryside into a house in Chelsea. His work on *Picture Post* had increased as changes were taking place as well as Gerti wishing to be nearer to London for her photographic work.

With both magazines running in tandem Hopkinson noted: "I had lost Charles Fenby, an assistant editor, who had transferred to another Hulton magazine, *The Leader*, which had recently been purchased. To replace Charles, I managed, with difficulty, to persuade Ted Castle to move from *The Daily Mirror*. Ted was a journalist of wide experience and many contacts; a good organiser who was liked by everyone."

"There were other losses in due course. Mac Hastings, returning from Europe, took over as editor of *Strand Magazine*; Anne Scott-James returned to a fashion publication, and Maurice Edelman, back from North Africa, was now in Parliament."

Hopkinson reflected: "One I was anxious to retain was Edgar Ainsworth, the art editor, whose job it was to work out the layouts for the various pages of both magazines. He was an excellent draughtsman who had come to us by way of advertising. Having lost so many good people to other employment, I was not willing to lose him too. He had been offered a job in an advertising agency but a pay increase made him stay on."

"He was then supported in his layout work by the newly appointed Assistant Art Editor, Rosemary Grimble, who would later make a name for herself by her exquisite line drawings. For a few months longer we hung on as best we could, and then back from the army came Lionel Birch and our ace photographer Bert Hardy."

"Sydney Jacobson wanted something closer to political life than *Lilliput* could offer so he moved to *Picture Post* as a trouble-shooting special correspondent, while Richard Bennett took over the editorship of *Lilliput*.

Richard Bennett was born in London and after graduating from Trinity College, Cambridge he joined the Hulton Group to work on various of their magazine titles. He was at the beginning of *Picture Post* staying until 1940, with his war service being spent mainly as the editor of the Army's *Bureau of Current Affairs*. In early 1946 he was recruited by Tom Hopkinson to join the editorial staff of *Lilliput* and six months later he became editor. This followed Hopkinson's internal transfer to be the full-time editor of *Picture Post*. In later years Bennett was to move to the editorial side of *The Sunday Telegraph*.

He made few changes when he took over the hot seat and soon had the benefit of an easing on paper restrictions. This allowed *Lilliput* to increase its pages to one hundred and twenty, of which twenty were advertisements. He made minor alterations to the contents and contributors' pages but the main body of the magazine remained unchanged. Another benefit was not having to commute to Northampton where *Lilliput* had been printed during the later years of the war.

Bennett had to be very diplomatic in the office as he knew that Kaye Webb had approached Maxwell Raison about becoming a joint-editor and her request had been summarily rejected. Also, Webb had been refused an office of her own which tended to make her moods rather gloomy. However, once she started an affair with the illustrator Ronald Searle things perked up as did the whole ambience of the office when Patrick Campbell came on the scene.

In his autobiography Campbell recalled: "Richard Bennett, the editor of *Lilliput* magazine, asked me to come and see him with a view to writing an occasional piece. After we had talked we had lunch together and then I went back with him to the office. By the time the pubs opened that evening he had offered me a regular job at one-thousand pounds a year salary, as an associate editor, plus twenty guineas for anything I wrote for the magazine."

"Bennett added that the rest of my work would be caption-writing and editing the work of outside contributors. This would leave me, he explained generously, as much time as I wanted for my weekly column in the *Sunday Dispatch* which I could write in the office, if I liked."

"If I had invented it myself I could not have thought of a better job. *Lilliput*, in those days, was still its crisp, satirical, intelligent and very funny self. The other senior members of staff - Kaye Webb, James Boswell, Mechthild Nawiasky, Maurice Richardson and John Symonds - were individually clever and more professional than anyone I had ever worked with before."

Campbell wrote later: "Of course, working for *Lilliput* did not feel like work at all. The office was in an alley overlooking a bomb-site, well away from the management's headquarters in Shoe Lane, and they, in any case, were much more concerned with *Picture Post*, the leading magazine in the Hulton group. It almost seemed that we owned *Lilliput* ourselves, that we could do exactly as we liked with it. There were no set conferences. We wandered in and out of one another's offices, presenting the most extraordinary ideas for the coming issue."

Meanwhile, in order to pacify Kaye Webb, Bennett sent her to Paris in order to see French photographers. She also prepared a broadcast for the BBC about cafe society (The Flore was the favourite of Sarte and Picasso, she reported) and on the impact of clothes rationing on Parisian chic.

Some months later, in May 1947, she was sent to New York by Tom Hopkinson. He wanted her to find the photographer Gjon Mili "an off-hand and indolent sort of chap" and to "tear a pile of Kodachromes away from him." With her parents in America, Webb stayed longer than anticipated, returning in late October. During this time Bennett had kept in touch with her mainly passing on office news and exchanging opinions.

Richard Bennett was quick to develop a more strictly British humour in the magazine. The leading spirits in this move were Patrick Campbell and Maurice Richardson. The first providing an adroit comedy of wit with the latter being notable for both the Lemuel Gulliver column and stories of surrealist humour involving a dwarf named Engelbrecht.

Short story writers were given space in a publication which was now a rival to *Punch* in its brand of English humour and definitely a cut above general interest periodicals in its literary contributions. *Lilliput*, alas, had not generally maintained its pre-war international range of contributors although the work of Belgian crime writer Georges Simenon regularly appeared from March 1947 in a series of fifteen-hundred word stories.

The July 1947 number saw the tenth anniversary of the magazine and the fact was noted by a short article on a rear page which was illustrated by a typical Ronald Searle cartoon. Titled 'A Happy Birthday to Us,' and written by Patrick Campbell, it said: "As soon as we saw the birthday coming we decided to do something about it. But what were we going to do? A tiny cake for every reader? A paper cap, perhaps, with every copy? A signed photograph of each member of the staff? A discouraging prospect if you study the staff. There were practical difficulties. We considered that the anniversary must be celebrated purely in a verbal form."

"We were sorry to abandon the idea of the tiny cake. What was going to take its place? We lay downwards in darkened rooms, concentrating, and then an altogether new problem crept up upon us, and presented itself for solution. Where, if we did find suitable words in which to celebrate our birthday, were we going to put them? Certainly not on the first page; that would have been altogether too flamboyant. Somewhere in the middle? They might have been overwhelmed. Finally, we hit upon this pitch. The last full editorial page of this issue."

"The last full page, then, was the place to take our stand. This page, in fact, is the place where we have taken our stand, and here we make the announcement that we are ten today, and thank you for your past support."

"By Jove, Digby, just as our housemaster predicted!"

June 1940

"No! Let's talk about the secret anti-tank gun afterwards"

August 1940

"Of course, if you do that you leave your left flank open."

August 1941

"And if the cleaner does all you say, I will remove the spell"

February 1941

27

Germany's Amateur Smugglers

by Michael Graham

In an effort to maintain the mark at its old value, Hitler some time ago decreed that no capital could be taken out of Germany. Many wealthy citizens, alarmed by the growing insecurity at home, racked their brains to find means of evading the law. Typical of the ingenious methods used are the following:

There appeared recently in the German official government newspaper an advertisement stating that a director of one of the large steel companies was looking for a private secretary. Applications with full details should be sent to such-and-such a box number at the newspaper's offices. A few hours after this advertisement appeared, the telephone rang at the offices of the paper and a gentleman explained that he was the man who had inserted the advert. Unfortunately, he said, he had to go to Switzerland on business and would they mind forwarding all the applications that came in the next few days to his address there?

The very next day this gentleman received his package in Zurich. The frontier officials of course knew that the official paper would not think of smuggling out either money or treasonable remarks about Hitler, so the letters had passed untouched. At the Zurich hotel the addressee opened the package, threw about two-hundred of the letters away without even looking at them, opened the other two-hundred carefully and removed the bundles of money which he had, himself, sent to the Nazi newspaper.

Another man deposited his will with a notary public in Berlin with instructions in large letters on the envelope: "Not to be opened until my death." A few months later he went abroad to a country near Germany. One day he dropped into the Nazi Consulate and explained that he would like to change his will, but that his doctor considered him too ill to take the trip back to Germany. Would the consul be so kind as to bring the envelope containing his will back with him from his next trip to Germany? The consul said he would. It was only after he had delivered the envelope and it was opened before his startled eyes that he discovered the enormity of his kindness. He, a Nazi consul (who was not bothered by frontier officials) had unknowingly smuggled out of Germany a fortune of almost a million marks.

Perhaps the shrewdest and most original scheme was thought out by still another amateur smuggler. A short time ago the worried Dr Schacht, president of the Reichsbank, announced that there would be no punishment for smugglers of money if they would confess their crime and bring their money back into the country before a certain date. One morning a gentleman, evidently very nervous, appeared at the office designated for these confessions and admitted that he had hidden away, in a safe in Zurich, the sum of fifty-thousand marks. The officials suggested that he tell them where the money was and they would instruct the consul in Zurich to get it back. That was the difficulty, the gentleman explained. The Zurich bank would not let anyone open his safe unless he was present. But he would willingly go to Zurich and return with the money. This seemed a little unwise to the officials. What assurance had they that he would return at all? So they compromised. The gentleman would go to Zurich with one Nazi official accompanying him. And since he liked to travel in comfort they would go in the gentleman's car.

They passed the frontier with no difficulty, the presence of a Nazi official assuring the customs men that everything inside was satisfactory. But as soon as they had covered a few miles of Swiss territory the gentleman stopped the car, opened the door and said to the surprised official: "Get out of my car. You can tell your people in Berlin that I have no safe and no money in Zurich, but I do have my entire fortune hidden away in this car. Thanks to your presence the customs men thought it unnecessary to search."

July 1937

The Fortune Teller

by Karel Capek

Everybody who knows anything about the subject will realise that this episode could not have happened in Czechoslovakia, or in France, or in Germany, for in all these countries, as you are aware, judges are bound to try offenders and to sentence them in accordance with the letter of the law and not in accordance with their shrewd common-sense and the dictates of their consciences. And the fact that in this story there is a judge who, in passing sentence, was guided not by the statute-book but by sound common-sense, is due to the circumstance that the incident which I am about to relate could have happened nowhere else than in England; in fact, it happened in London, or to be more precise, in Bayswater. The judge was, as a matter of fact, a magistrate, and his name was Kelly. Also there was a lady, and her name was plain Edith Myers. Well, I must tell you that this lady, who was otherwise a respectable person, came under the notice of Detective-Inspector MacLeary.

"My dear," said MacLeary to his wife one evening, "I can't get that Mrs Myers out of my head. What I'd like to know, is how the woman makes her living. Just fancy, here we are in the month of February and she's sent her servant for asparagus. And I've discovered that she has between twelve and twenty visitors every day, and they vary from charwomen to duchesses. I know, darling, you'll say she's probably a fortune-teller. Very likely, but that can only be a blind for something else, say, the white slave traffic or espionage. Look here, I'd rather like to get to the bottom of it."

"All right, Bob," said the excellent Mrs MacLeary, "you leave it to me." And so it came about that on the following day, Mrs MacLeary, of course without her wedding ring, but on the other hand very girlishly dressed and with her hair in ringlets like a young woman who feels that it is time for her to put away frivolities, with a scared look on her baby face, rang at Mrs Myers' door in Bayswater. She had to wait quite a while before Mrs Myers received her.

"Sit down, my dear," said the old lady, when she had very thoroughly inspected her shy visitor. "What can I do for you?" "I - I" stammered Mrs MacLeary. "I'd like - it's my twentieth birthday tomorrow - I'm awfully anxious to know about my future." "But, Miss—er, what name, please?" asked Mrs Myers, and seized a pack of cards which she began to shuffle energetically. "Jones," sighed Mrs MacLeary. "My dear Miss Jones," continued Mrs Myers, "you're quite mistaken, I don't tell fortunes by cards, except, of course, just now and then, to oblige a friend, as every old woman does. Take the cards in your left hand and divide them into five heaps. That's right. Sometimes I read the cards as a pastime, but apart from that—dear me!" she said, cutting the first heap. "Diamonds. That means money. And the knave of hearts. That's a nice hand."

"Ah," said Mrs MacLeary, "and what else?" "Knave of diamonds," proceeded Mrs Myers, uncovering the second heap. "Ten of spades, that's a journey. But here" she exclaimed. "I see clubs. Clubs always means worry, but there's a queen of hearts at the bottom."

"What does that mean?" asked Mrs MacLeary, opening her eyes as wide as she could. "Diamonds again," meditated Mrs Myers over the third heap. "My dear, there's lots of money in store for you; but I can't tell whether you're going on a long journey or whether it's someone near and dear to you." "I've got to go to Southampton to see my aunt," remarked Mrs MacLeary. "That must be the long journey," said Mrs Myers, cutting the fourth heap. "Somebody's going to get in your way, some elderly man." "I expect that's my uncle!" exclaimed Mrs MacLeary.

"Well, here we've got something and no mistake," declared Mrs Myers over the fifth heap. "My dear Miss Jones, this is the nicest hand I've ever seen. There will be a wedding before the year's out; a very, very rich young man is going to marry you. He must be a millionaire or a businessman, because he travels a lot; but before you are united, you'll have to overcome great obstacles, there's an elderly gentleman who'll get in your way, but you must persevere. When you do get married, you'll move a long way off, most likely across the ocean. My fee's a guinea, for the Christian mission to the poor negroes."

"I'm so grateful to you," declared Mrs MacLeary, taking one pound and one shilling out of her handbag, "awfully grateful. Mrs Myers, what would it cost without any of those worries?" "The cards can't be bribed," said the old lady with dignity. "What is your uncle?" "He's in the police," lied the young lady with an innocent face. "You know, the secret service."

"Oh!" said the old lady, and drew three cards out of the heap. "That's very nasty, very nasty. Tell him, my dear, that he's threatened by a great danger. He ought to come and see me, to find out more about it. There's lots of them from Scotland Yard come here and get me to read the cards for them, and they all tell me what they have on their minds. Yes, just you send him to me. You say he's on secret service work? Mr Jones? Tell him I'll be expecting him. Goodbye, Miss Jones. Next, please!"

"I don't like the look of this," said Mr MacLeary, scratching his neck reflectively. "I don't like the look of this, Katie. That woman has too much interested in your late uncle. Besides that, her real name isn't Myers, but Meierhofer, and she hails from Lubeck. A damned German!" growled MacLeary. "I wonder how we can stop her little game? I wouldn't mind betting five to one that she worms things out of people that are no business of hers. I'll tell you what; I'll pass the word on to the bosses."

And MacLeary did, in good faith, pass the word on to the bosses. Oddly enough, the bosses took a serious view of the matter, and so it came about that the worthy Mrs Myers was summoned to appear before Mr Kelly.

"Well, Mrs Myers," the magistrate said to her, "what's all this I hear about this fortune-telling of yours with cards?" "Good gracious, your worship," said the old lady, "I must do something for a living. At my age I can't go on the music-halls and dance!"

"Hm," said Kelly. "But the charge against you is that you don't read the cards properly. My dear good lady, that's as bad as if you were to give people slabs of clay when they ask for cakes of chocolate. In return for a fee of one guinea people are entitled to a correct prophecy. Look here now, what's the good of your trying to prophesy when you don't know how to?"

"It isn't everyone who complains," urged the old lady in her defence. "You see, I foretell the things they like. The pleasure they get out of it is worth a few shillings. And sometimes I'm right. Mrs Myers, said one lady to me, nobody's ever read the cards for me as well as you have and given me such good advice. She lives in St. John's Wood and is getting a divorce from her husband."

"Look here," the magistrate cut her short. "We've got a witness against you. Mrs MacLeary, tell the court what happened." "Mrs Myers told me from the cards," began Mrs MacLeary glibly, "that before the year was out I'd be married, that my future husband would be a rich young man and that I'd go with him across the ocean. "

"Why across the ocean particularly?" inquired the magistrate. "Because there was the nine of spades in the second heap; Mrs Myers said that means journeys."

"Rubbish!" growled the magistrate. "The nine of spades means hope. It's the jack of spades that means journeys; and when it turns up with the seven of diamonds, that means long journeys that are likely to lead to something worthwhile. Mrs Myers, you can't bamboozle me. You prophesied to the witness here that before the year was out she'd marry a rich young man. But Mrs MacLeary has been married for the last three years to Detective-Inspector MacLeary, and a fine fellow he is too. Mrs Myers, how do you explain that absurdity?"

"My goodness me!" said the old lady placidly. "That does happen now and then. When this young person called on me she was all dressed up, but her left glove was torn. So that looked as if she wasn't too well off," but she wanted to make a show all the same. Then she said she was twenty, but now it turns out she's twenty-five." "Twenty-four," Mrs MacLeary burst forth.

"That's all the same. Well, she wanted to get married, what I mean to say, she made out to me she wasn't married. So I arranged a set of cards for her that would mean a wedding and a rich husband. I thought that would meet the case better than anything else."

"And what about the obstacles, the elderly gentleman and the journey across the ocean?" asked Mrs MacLeary. "That was to give you plenty for your money," said Mrs Myers artlessly. "There's quite a lot has to be told for a guinea."

"Well, that's enough," said the magistrate. "Mrs Myers, it's no use. The way you tell fortunes by cards is a fraud. Cards take some understanding. Of course, there are various ideas about it, but if my memory serves me, the nine of spades never means journeys. You'll pay a fine of fifty pounds, just the same as people who adulterate food or sell worthless goods. There's a suspicion, too, Mrs Myers, that you're engaged in espionage as well. But I don't expect you'll admit that." "As true as I'm standing here." exclaimed Mrs Myers.

But Kelly interrupted her. "Well, we'll say no more about that. But as you're an alien without any proper means of subsistence, the authorities will make use of the powers vested in them, and will have you deported. Goodbye, Mrs Myers, and thank you Mrs MacLeary. I must say that this inaccurate fortune-telling is a disgraceful and unscrupulous business. Just bear that in mind, Mrs Myers." "What am I to do now?" sighed the old lady. "Just when I was beginning to get a good connection together."

About a year later Kelly met Detective-Inspector MacLeary. "Fine weather," said the magistrate amiably. "By the way, how is Mrs MacLeary?" MacLeary looked very glum. "Well; you know, Mr. Kelly," he said with a certain embarrassment, "Mrs MacLeary——well, the fact is, she's left me." "You don't say so," said the magistrate in astonishment, "such a nice young lady, too!"

"That's just it," growled MacLeary. "Some young whipper-snapper went crazy about her before I knew what was happening. He's a millionaire, or a businessman from Melbourne. I tried to stop her, but ..." MacLeary made a helpless gesture with his hand, "a week ago they sailed together for Australia."

October 1937

Love By Post

by Kathleen Hewitt

The mail went every fortnight. Sometimes Evelyn wrote ten pages, sometimes fifteen, and on occasions as many as twenty. John, her husband, was four thousand miles away, on a road-making job in the African Bush. It was understood that she could not be expected to go out to him. There were too many dangers; malaria, sleeping sickness, the climate. So, John declared, her letters were all he had to cheer him in the two-year stretches he was away from her.

She used to leave it till the day the mail went to start writing. But as John liked to think she penned a line or so every day she would insert successive dates, so that the whole screed was broken into instalments that, as often as not, ended "more tomorrow, darling." Several times she almost missed the mail. Once, owing to a prolonged party, she did miss it and had to dash to Euston to give her letter to a man who was catching the boat train, so that he could post it on board and ensure its getting there on the right day. She owed it to him not to fail; besides, if he did not hear he would want explanations.

"My sweetest Evelyn," John replied, "it was just wonderful of you to send such a heavenly letter, and so brave of you to despatch it as you did, rushing to the station when you'd been too ill to get out and post it." Only once did she slip up badly, forgetting the mail until even the ship had sailed. So she cabled: "Sorry missed writing owing to influenza love Evelyn."

That ought to have kept him quiet. Instead, the anxious fool cabled back to his sister, "Evelyn ill send me news," and she herself had had to pretend to be a convalescent when actually she was bursting with health

33

and furious at missing a party. Still, it was worth it. For two years she was a grass widow with a good allowance. Then she would have four months of John, made fairly tolerable by his splashing the money he hadn't been able to spend in the African Bush.

There came a day when Evelyn felt that the strain of correspondence was almost too great. John's replies never lacked enthusiasm; indeed, she sometimes thought, he ought to have been a romantic poet, so flowery were his phrases: "My lovely, lovely wife! I sit and think of you till your face becomes a mirage against the tropical night sky. In my dreams I hear your voice. . . ."

Evelyn said to her friend Diana Barr: "It's too much. I can't keep it up. I'll have to write and tell him so, and he'll have to be content with an odd line or so when I feel inclined to scribble it." Diana, Eton cropped, slick, the very competent secretary to Savile Estates, Ltd., warned her: "He'll never stand for it. You've got to remember your cheque on the first of the month. After all, writing a few pages isn't much to do to earn it."

"The whole thing's getting on my nerves," Evelyn insisted, "and his answers make me want to go screeching down Piccadilly." Diana wrinkled her resourceful brow. "He types his, doesn't he?" "Always. He bought a portable from a man on the same job." "Well, why shouldn't you learn to type too?"

"For pity's sake, Diana. Is that going to make the strain any easier?" "Yes," Diana said. "Because all you'll have to do is to dictate your drivel to me and I'll take it down and run it off on the machine. Mustn't let him know of course, that there's any collaboration." "That's a brainwave!" Evelyn agreed. "You're a gem. It'll only take us half an hour a fortnight.'

The idea worked admirably. Gradually Diana got to know Evelyn's chatty style so well that with John's last effusion to refer to, she could write the whole thing and all Evelyn had to do was to scrawl her signature and a row of kisses at the bottom. If anything, the letters were more affectionate than before, and nowadays were never less than twenty pages long. Once, after a cocktail party, Diana knocked off thirty. John's replies grew even more enthusiastic.

"It just shows you," Evelyn contended, "that a bit of planning works wonders. I don't have to sit chewing a pen, John thinks I adore him more than ever, and poor darling, he does appreciate my devotion. So everyone's happy."

In his bush bungalow, a hundred miles from the nearest railhead, John groaned as his dusky steward boy brought in his mail. Another interminable yarn from Evelyn. She meant well, of course. He reflected that writing must take up the dickens of a lot of her time. Still, perhaps not so much since she'd learnt to use a typewriter. He left the package unopened until Hopkins, his second-in-command, came over for a drink. "There you are," John said. "Another little lump of verbal emotion for

34

you to deal with. Make the answer nice and fruity, lots of endearments and plenty of our damn fool pet names sprinkled in." "It's all very well," Hopkins growled, "but it's the very devil keeping up your old standards. Still, I'll do what I can, old man." He began to open the envelope.

"Funny, I'm the only thing Evelyn cares about in the whole wide world," said John. "Can't blame her for spilling her affection in ink. I daresay it comforts her, sitting and writing in her lonely evenings. So knock off a decent instalment for this mail, there's a good chap. Lashings of the love-hunger dope. You know what's needed." Hopkins pulled out the thickly folded pages. He glanced at the first and exclaimed, "Holy smoke. What's this?" "What's the matter? Not ill again, is she? If so I'll have to cable my sister again. Bit of fussing makes Evelyn feel good."

Hopkins began to read: "'Dear Sirs; With reference to your inquiry re the Mayland property we have to inform you that the land in question covers an area of twenty-two acres. It's addressed from Savile Estates, Ltd. The answer to this," he added drily. "doesn't seem to call for many endearments."

An elderly gentleman in Mayfair opened the only letter the postman had brought. He was expecting an answer to his inquiry about a country estate he thought of buying. So naturally he was startled as he read: "My own adored precious, your too-too heavenly letter has arrived, and hugging it to my heart I am sending you love, hugs, and kisses. . . . My poppet is lonely and so am I; just trembling for the moment I shall hold you in my arms --."

The old gentleman was unable to send any sort of reply, because he had an apoplectic fit on his handsome Persian carpet. And his wife had violent hysterics when she perused the twenty passionate pages from some shameless wanton, obviously her husband's mistress, whose existence she had never even suspected.

November 1937

A Viennese Cameo

by Lajos Biro

The streets of Vienna were swept by sharp spring breezes. The three Scholz boys, all members of the Court Theatre orchestra, came out of the theatre, turned up their coat-collars, and gloomily started for home. There they were met by their mother, a grey, crushed old woman, who humbly took their cloaks from them, then hurried into the kitchen to get their supper.

The three Scholz boys sat at the table glumly. "Isn't father home yet?" asked Rudolf through his teeth. "No, he hasn't come home yet," replied his mother with humble haste. Rudolf began to eat. His mother waited a little, but, as usual, none of her sons deigned to speak to her, so she mutely and humbly slunk back to the kitchen. The three boys ate in gloomy silence. Then Franz passed his hand over his long hair and sighed: "I can't bear it any longer." Maximilian shook his leonine head. "I'm going to leave them," he said in his deep voice, resonant with pain. "I know of a good room," put in Rudolf, "near the bastion. The house belongs to a pastry cook; he has some pretty daughters." "We'll move there, then," said Maximilian.

They continued to eat, sunk in thought. Towards the end of the meal, they heard their father's voice from outside, so they finished hastily, retired to their room, and lighting their pipes lay down each on his own bed.

Meanwhile their father, Herr Scholz, a retired usher of the Imperial Court, slowly but noisily entered the dining-room. He had, that evening, lingered very long in the company of his cronies. They spoke about the outbreak of a revolution in Paris, and reviled Metternich without restraint. This talk had so roused the former Imperial servant that he had in his agitation consumed even more wine than usual.

By the time he was seated at the table his wife was already bringing his supper from the kitchen, yet he started to grumble. "Of course, Lizi, you'd be happy if I died of starvation. You'd like to bury me, Lizi, eh? But it's no use, Lizi, I'm going to bury you, Lizi. I'll see you dead, if it's the last thing I see in this life."

The woman placed the dishes on the table tremblingly and humbly. "You're trembling?" barked Herr Scholz, "trembling? Why didn't you tremble then? But then it was only your sinful body that was writhing, not your soul." Shaking like a leaf, the woman drew away from the table and attempted to slink back into the kitchen. "Stop" he barked. The woman stopped. Herr Scholz ate and drank, talking between mouthfuls.

"'I see you're praying," he said. "But it's no use you praying. You're going to burn in hell anyhow. But before I send you there you'll have to atone here in this world for having betrayed your lawful husband. For having broken the vows you made at the altar. For having besmirched the sacrament of marriage. Stand there, you. Don't move. Your atonement has lasted for twenty-two years; in another ten years I'll send you to meet your judge; but until then I'll go on punishing you. Providence has placed the task in my hands and I'll. . . ."

In the adjoining room the three boys tossed restlessly on their beds. "He's going to beat her again," said Rudolf in a low voice. Maximilian

36

shrugged his shoulders. "Aren't you used to it yet?" he said morosely. Franz's mouth twitched. "For twenty-two years" he said darkly. "It's a long time. She's suffered a great deal, but. . . ."

"We've had this all our lives," said Rudolf bitterly. "But we'll suffer much longer," completed Maximilian, "for the shame she's brought on us." "No one knows," said Franz defiantly. "It's enough if we know it," replied Maximilian grimly.

He flung himself off the bed and walked up and down in the room in fierce agitation. Meanwhile, in the dining-room the ex-court usher had finished his supper and was getting ready to beat his wife. "On your knees," he barked, "on your knees before the husband you've wronged. Do you admit that you've been unfaithful to me?" "Yes," breathed the trembling woman. "How many lovers did you have?" "One. I swear it." "Who was he?"

The woman with a low swooning moan told him. Maximilian stood trembling behind the door. Suddenly he tossed his leonine head; his face was pale as he turned to his brothers, who lay on their beds with pain and vexation on their faces. "Did you hear the name?" he panted. "No," replied his brothers.

Maximilian quickly told them. Rudolf and Franz leapt to their feet. The three brothers looked at each other with burning eyes and for a moment stood motionless, shocked into immobility. In the dining-room the ex-court usher rose to his feet and braced himself for the beating with circumstance and satisfaction. "Well," he said, savouring the words, "if that was who it was, then I'll . . ."

He raised his arm. But at this moment the door crashed open and Maximilian burst in. The upraised arm of the ex-court usher was gripped by an angry hand. "Leave her alone," snapped Maximilian, "she's had enough." "Is that how I taught you to behave?" shouted Herr Scholz indignantly. "No," said Maximilian, "it isn't. But we've had enough of this."

Herr Scholz tried to release his arm and strike his wife, but Maximilian held it firmly. "How dare you raise your hand against your own father," croaked Herr Scholz. "The hand that a child raises against his parent is cursed." "Then leave her alone." "She broke the vows she made before the altar." "She's suffered enough for it," said Rudolf. "Why didn't you send her away?" said Franz angrily. "If you've kept her, don't torment her."

The ex-court usher wanted to mete out punishment at all costs, and struggled to free himself. But his three sons seized him, bundled him into the third room and turned the key. The outraged Herr Scholz made two swift attacks on the door, then he lay down on the bed and fell asleep. In the middle of the dining-room the woman, with tears in her eyes, her humble bearing unchanged, was smoothing down her skirt. Her three sons, deeply confused, stood around her.

"Sit down, Mother," said Maximilian at length, with embarrassment in his deep voice. "Sit down with us," said Rudolf. Franz pushed a chair in front of her. They made her sit at the head of the table, then they too sat down. But for a time they were unable to speak. The three boys had grown up despising their mother and intimate talk and warm words came hard to them now. The woman's sorrowful, frightened eyes darted searchingly from one son to the other. The boys lowered their gaze. At length, Maximilian raised his leonine head and said: "Mother, did I hear right what you said just now?"

"What?" "That name, the name of the man with whom ... who was it?" The woman's tired eyelids shut over her wet eyes. "Beethoven," she whispered. The three boys exchanged startled glances. "Which Beethoven?" asked Maximilian with a gulp in his dry throat. The woman's faded eyelids opened again. "There was only one," she replied in a low voice.

"Ludwig von Beethoven?" asked Maximilian in an awed whisper. "Ludwig von Beethoven," replied his mother. "When we were living in the same house. That was why I raised you all to be musicians." There was silence in the room. The three boys were shocked into muteness. Then they drew closer to their mother, timidly stroked her dress, and Rudolf in a moved, melting voice said: "Mother . . . tell us." "Tell us about him," said Franz.

Maximilian with knitted brows gently nodded his head. The woman looked at them. Then she gazed into the distance and slowly a soft light came into her eyes. In a tremulous, dreamy voice she began to talk, and the three musicians listened with bated breath, hungrily, reverently, with deep emotion.

November 1937

Proposal By Proxy

by Kathleen Hewitt

Nearly all the guests of *The Limes* had gone away for Christmas. In this suburban boarding establishment there remained only Miss Salter, Mr Dodd, and the two student brothers, Jerry and Joe O'Sullivan. The four of them sat in the drawing-room after lunch on Christmas Eve. Across the ceiling hung bells of crimson paper that somehow looked more melancholy than gay. The old-fashioned pictures were trimmed with holly and a single stalk of mistletoe hung on the central chandelier.

Mr Dodd said: "Ah, the festive season. Our landlady makes it as gay as she can." Mr Dodd was in his forties. He had a scholarly stoop and courtly manners. Though slightly shabby, for teachers of mathematics are not overpaid, Miss Salter thought him very distinguished. "Christmas," she said, "always takes one's mind back. I remember when I was a girl, what fun we had."

Mr Dodd nodded, though it was hard to associate Miss Salter with fun. Thin, almost gaunt, she was dressed primly. Her auburn hair was touched with grey; but she had large light blue eyes that, Mr Dodd thought, would be lovely even when she was really old.

Joe O'Sullivan winked at Jerry. They both rose. "We've got a spot of shopping to do," Joe said. "We've left it, as usual, to the last moment." They tumbled out of the room like eager puppies. "Nice lads," Mr Dodd remarked. "They don't take their studies very seriously." As she spoke Miss Salter reflected that she, who had taken life seriously enough, had not made much of it.

Mr Dodd said: "I'll be glad when the holiday's over. It isn't so gay when one's middle-aged. Though of course you'll always be ......" "What?" she asked, smiling encouragement. He had not sufficient daring to say what was in his mind. Looking at the sheen on Miss Salter's red-brown hair one forgot the suspicion of grey. Her fine skin, her quick smile, most of all her eyes, made her beautiful.

"Miss Salter" he began, and stopped, appalled that even for a second he should have thought of telling her the truth, that he loved her. He would never have the courage to ask her to marry him. "Yes, Mr Dodd?" "I was only thinking; it's strange that anyone like you should be alone at this time."

"This isn't like a home of one's own, but I'm certainly not lonely, Mr Dodd." Miss Salter moved her chair slightly. It brought her directly under the mistletoe, but he seemed not to notice. She had always been proud of the fact that men took no liberties with her. And yet, how much more thrilling life would be if sometimes they did. Mr Dodd said fervently: "Well, that's very charming of you." He might have continued, but Mrs Bourne, their plump and motherly landlady, came bustling in, and a triangular conversation trailed along until teatime.

Meanwhile, Jerry and Joe O'Sullivan, roaming aimlessly, for they had come out merely to escape from the drawing room at *The Limes*, found themselves at the entrance of a sixpenny bazaar. They drifted in with the cheerful crowds. "We ought to get Mrs Bourne a present," Joe said. "Have a heart! You know how broke we are."

"Then this is our shop. What about one of these Union Jack calendars? It ought to please her patriotic tastes." "Right, a calendar for Mrs Bourne. Aren't we going to give old Dodd anything?" They were in a lively mood. They chose, for the solemn teacher, a vase in the shape of a heart on which was printed in gold 'To My Love.' As the girl wrapped it up, Jerry said: "There's still Miss Salter. What about her?" "Perfume," Joe exclaimed. "Look at this, Bouquet d'Amour, all for a tanner." He picked up the bottle, tapping his coin on the counter. They laughed gleefully as they left the bazaar.

Christmas morning found them in a more sober mood, somewhat diffident, indeed, about offering their gifts. The calendar for Mrs Bourne, that was all right. But, the heart-shaped vase; the Bouquet d'Amour? The other two might not take their cheek in good humour. It was Jerry who had the brainwave, and who wrote the messages to accompany the two gifts. A good idea, Joe agreed, an excellent joke to enliven a day that threatened to be somewhat dull.

Miss Salter, as usual, came punctually to breakfast. Mr Dodd arrived a moment later, in time to speculate as to why, having opened the packet beside her plate, Miss Salter should flush so warmly and throw him a coy glance across the breakfast table. Mr Dodd, too, found a small package addressed to him. He adjusted his pince-nez to open it, and on a slip of paper he read: "From Susan Salter. Merry Xmas. Reading the inscription on the vase, Mr Dodd was so excited that he dipped his elbow right into his poached egg, and Mrs Bourne had to run about finding a cloth to wipe his coat.

A quarter of an hour later Miss Salter was alone in the drawing room. Mr Dodd entered and went straight to her with a boldness he had never before shown. "How kind of you, Susan," he exclaimed. "I shall keep it all my life." "Keep what? But I must thank you. I'm not used to scent, so I appreciate it all the more." Miss Salter leaned forward; from the lacy collar of her frock he caught the perfume. A crude odour, it was true, but he was thinking more of how tender her eyes were. "Thank you, Mr Dodd."

"For what?" Really, Miss Salter reflected, the man was absurdly shy, though he had given her so significant a gift. "For," she hesitated, "for the 'flowers of love.'" "The flowers" Mr Dodd, completely mystified, broke off abruptly. Then he realised that they were standing right under the hanging stalk of mistletoe, and Miss Salter's attitude was so confiding, so inviting, that he lost all his nervousness and kissed her bravely on the lips.

In the hall Joe said to Jerry: "They're bound to find out who did it, and then they'll give us hell."

Kissing Miss Salter was pleasant. Mr. Dodd did it again. They did not want to give anyone hell; two shy, lonely people were discovering an unexpected heaven.

January 1938

Miranda Finds A New Career

by Rhoda Somervell

Her friends, and Miranda had many friends, always agreed that she had a gay courage which would pull her through most emergencies. Who but she, they asked, would have presented so smiling a face to the world when her husband eloped with her best friend, and her income vanished in the slump?

Only Miranda would have closed her luxurious home and taken an attic flat in which she arranged what was left of her furniture after the sale, and then set out to look for work, with never a sigh of self-pity. Only Miranda would have the courage to live in the old, draughty office building which, at night, was deserted. "After all," said her friends, "she's still got some decent jewellery, and furs, and things, and there are burglars." At which Miranda laughed and said: "One day I'll get a watchdog, and, anyway, I've got the only key."

But there came a night when such warnings suddenly occurred to her. It struck three as she climbed up the dark stairs and inserted her key in the lock. And in that moment someone switched out a light in her sitting room. Miranda paused. She was in evening clothes and wearing her jewellery. She was tired, and wished she had not left the young man who had escorted her home on her doorstep.

Even as she thought of her helplessness a voice barked at her: "Hands up." The light in the little hallway blazed up and she saw a masked man. Miranda obeyed instantly. "Now come in," he said. Feeling somewhat foolish with her arms above her head Miranda walked into her sitting room ahead of him as he switched on the light. She looked round to see that it was untouched. Even a little side table, on which were cigarettes, some whisky and a soda-syphon in case she had brought back a guest with her, was undisturbed.

"What do you want?" she asked. "You can take off that stuff you're wearing," he said. "Oh," she said. "Certainly, but what makes you think they're worth it?" "I've been watching you for a bit," he said. "You're not the sort to wear paste." Miranda laughed. "Is that a compliment? Well, if you insist, only there's something I must tell you first. Can I put my arms down?"

"If you don't try any tricks," he answered. She let her arms fall with a gesture of utter weariness. Then she sank down into a deep chair. "Pour me out a drink, will you?" she said, and even her voice had taken on the harshness of exhaustion. "Whisky and just a splash of soda. You've given me a shock, you know."

He looked at her and she saw his eyes bright and wary through the slits in the black handkerchief which concealed most of his face. "You're a rum 'un," he said, and advanced gingerly towards the little table. She opened her bag and extracted two white pellets which she held in her open palm.

"Give us the bag," he said. "Certainly," she agreed. "There's only half-a-crown in it, I'm afraid." As he held out the glass she took it and let him snatch the bag from her. When he looked at her again she swallowed the pellets and finished her drink, and said: "So you want my poor bits of jewellery. Well, I will give them to you in a minute. There's something I want to say first."

She hesitated. "It wouldn't be fair not to tell you. You may see for yourself that it'll be foolish." "What do you mean?" he said uneasily. "Hurry up." She held up one hand and stared at him intently. "You wouldn't like," she said very slowly, "to have them looking for you for more than robbery; for perhaps, murder?"

"Come off it," he snarled. "I shan't hurt you if you don't try any funny business." "I wasn't thinking of that," she said, and it seemed to him that her face had suddenly grown haggard. "I came back tonight to finish it all. I can't go on. It's the only way out for me."

" 'Ere," he looked at her uncertainly, "what's it all about?"

"I'm broke," she said. "As desperate as you. Only I'm hopeless. And I'm in a worse jam than you'd understand. Tomorrow when everyone knows, I shan't have a friend in the world, so I've made up my mind." He took a step nearer her. "Seems like you're barmy. Here give me the stuff, I'm off."

"Remember," she said, very quietly, "that if they catch you with anything, after they've found me here, dead, you may be accused of . . ." He laughed uncomfortably. "I've heard 'em talk that way before. Your sort always does over nothing. You can't scare me. Besides, them that talks so much never does it."

"You saw me take the stuff, just now," she reminded him. "Them pills" She nodded. Suddenly she gasped and rose to her feet, pressing her hands against her stomach. Then she swayed back against the fireplace. "Oh, they said it wouldn't hurt. Oh, the pain." He took a step backward. She gasped again and fell sprawling on the soft carpet, her body writhing.

"Oh . . . stop it. Get someone to stop it. . . . I can't stand it. . . ." Her voice rose in a hysterical scream. "Help . . . help," he cried, and then broke off, realising the stupidity of shouting. He shrank back as he realised that she was attempting to crawl towards him. She could no longer speak, she was only gasping, and then as if with a prodigious effort he heard her groan: "It'll be too late. Help. . . I'm going. . . . I'm going. . . ."

He saw her spine arch, and thought there was a froth on her lips. Her fingers dug into the soft pile of the carpet. There were diamonds glittering on her wrist and her bag was open on the table. He did not dare touch either. Panic overcame him. "You fool" he shouted down at her and rushed to the door. There was the sound of the front door slammed behind him, a soft padding as he fled down the stairs. Then a faint thud as the outer door of the building closed with more care.

Very slowly Miranda opened one eye. She was listening intently. She sat up very carefully, and a smile spread over her face. "Really," she said aloud, "I'm wasted in an office. I'd better try for the talkies."

February 1938

"Chap here says his name is Stone . . ."

March 1942

"Come in, Elsie, and show Mr. and Mrs. Harper how you strangle a man"

May 1944

"And I got the top one for rescuing a very old lady from the village duckpond"

March 1945

"So you mean you've actually spoken to Donald Duck?"

November 1945

Jubilee of Cleopatra's Needle

by Michael Corvin

Just sixty years ago a very strange vessel came up the River Thames to London, a steel cylinder equipped with the rigging of a normal ship. Inside the steel cylinder was the mighty obelisk that now stands on the Embankment and is called Cleopatra's Needle.

To start at the beginning, the name is wrong. The lovely and unhappy last Queen of Egypt had nothing whatever to do with this towering piece of granite. Moreover, there are two such 'needles,' the other graces a site in Central Park, New York.

Up to the beginning of the nineteenth century nobody bothered about the obelisk which the great King Thutmose had erected in Heliopolis some time about 1500 BC. The Emperor Augustus, in accordance with the Roman custom of using old statues to grace a triumph, had it brought to Alexandria and set up there with its twin, now in New York. The golden caps on the tips had been stolen long ago when an earthquake upset our obelisk in 1303 AD, and thus gave it the opportunity of spending the next five-hundred years in a horizontal position.

Then, however, its days of rest were over. Napoleon Bonaparte arrived with forty-thousand men and a strong fleet to conquer Egypt. Near Abukir the fleet met Horatio Nelson, and on land a decisive battle was fought in the immediate vicinity of the fallen obelisk.

That was the beginning of the saga of Cleopatra's Needle. The victorious English fleet and army wanted to bring a great and worthy souvenir of the event home to England and chose the obelisk. The soldiers and officers collected £7,000 for its transport, and plans were made to ship it to England. A pier was built, a sunken French frigate raised and repaired, the obelisk cleared of sand; but a storm destroyed the pier in a single night and wrecked the frigate. The army moved on, and Cleopatra's Needle again lay forgotten under a shroud of sand.

In 1818, Mohamed Ali, the viceroy, remembered the incident, and presented the stone to England on condition that the English would take it away themselves. In 1832 Parliament refused to grant a single penny for this purpose. In 1851 someone had the bright idea of bringing Cleopatra's Needle to London and setting it up as a memorial to the work done by Prince Albert in organising the Great Exhibition. But nothing came of it. Not until 1875 did things slowly start moving. A patron was found in Sir William Wilson, and an engineer, John Dixon, offered to undertake the transport. In January 1877, Dixon signed a contract to bring the obelisk to London.

A dozen different schemes were evolved to move the two-hundred ton stone. Finally, the most startling of all was adopted. This was to encase the whole seventy foot obelisk in a steel cylinder where it lay, drag the steel cylinder down to the sea, put rudder and rigging on it, and tow it behind a steamer to the River Thames.

The first part of this scheme offered no difficulties, and the great stone was successfully encased in the cylinder. On 28 August 1877, the whole contraption was dragged down to the sea by way of a specially constructed channel. A thick fog hampered operations. The cylinder was hard to move, but in the end it glided into the sea, only to be half submerged immediately. During the journey to the sea a stone had torn a leak in the cylinder.

With the greatest difficulty the cylinder was hauled out of the water again, repaired and refloated. In a dry dock belonging to the Khedive the cylinder was rigged up, and on 21 September 1877, the cylinder-ship, christened Cleopatra, set out in the wake of the steamship Olga. The Cleopatra seems to have been none too seaworthy, and despite additional ballast the stone in its inside caused it to roll most unpleasantly. Still, it passed the Straits of Gibraltar and rounded Cape St. Vincent on 10 October only to strike a terrible gale four days later. Let an eye-witness describe what followed.

"The Cleopatra rolled terribly, and the steel cables connecting her with the Olga cracked and sang in the storm. We kept clear of them as well as we could, and it was lucky we did so, for soon both cables broke almost simultaneously with a howling noise and the Cleopatra was alone. The cursed cylinder suddenly developed a list, the ballast shifted, and all our efforts to right it were in vain.

"Despite the weather the Olga kept close to us, but it was quite impossible to throw a line across. There we were in the raging storm with a list of more than forty-five degrees, in a ship which was not a ship at all. We were about one-hundred miles from Ferrol [Galicia], but there was not a shadow of a possibility for us to get there without assistance. Things looked bad indeed. We felt as if we were carrying our own tombstone, although we did not need any here. The skipper summoned all hands on deck. There was nothing for it but to lower our only boat and attempt to reach the Olga. But before the boat touched the water, a great wave dashed it against the cursed steel hull and shattered it to matchwood."

"We saw that the Olga lowered a boat and six men, all stout lads, rest their souls, jumped in. A wave lifted them up high, they gave way, and then something like a mountain of glass came rolling along, lifted the little boat up high, twisted it round, broke the oars, and then with a hellish roar swallowed everything in a whirlpool of foam. We never saw any of the six any more, not a single one of them so much as came up once.

"After that we gave up, but the captain of the Olga did not. He came alongside and threw us a line, despite the danger that we might strike her and cut her in two like a giant torpedo. One after the other we were hauled aboard, and not one of us so much as glanced back at the iron hulk with the stone in it. The storm lasted quite a while, and when we looked out for the Cleopatra she was nowhere to be seen. We did not mourn very much for her being sunk."

But the Cleopatra had not sunk. The cylinder was airtight and held. A few days later the Fitzmaurice sighted her seventy miles out of Ferrol, took her in tow and brought her to Ferrol, where she lay for the next three months. Finally, on 20 January 1878, the stone reached the Thames in the wake of the tug Anglia. At first, more thought was given to the six victims lying at the bottom of the Bay of Biscay than to the obelisk.

Then, after a dispute about the site on which the monolith was to be erected, the Metropolitan Board of Works decided that Cleopatra's Needle should stand on the Embankment. A pedestal was erected and the Victorian Age deposited its visiting card in a hollow inside. It is worth noting what was at the time considered important and worthy to be preserved in the great earthenware chests under the obelisk.

A standard foot measure and pound weight; a small bronze model of the obelisk; a document printed on silk describing the transport of the obelisk to London; a splinter from the base of the obelisk; a set of British coins; a rupee; a copy of the translation by Wallis Budgen of the hieroglyphic inscription on the stone; a portrait of Queen Victoria; Bibles in several languages; a Hebrew Pentateuch; the Arabian Genesis; a part of the Gospel according to St. John; a Bradshaw railway timetable; a shilling razor; a box of cigars; tobacco pipes; hairpins; jewellery; a baby's milk-bottle and toys; a set of hydraulic lifting tackle; lengths of steel cable and deep-sea cables; a map of London; copies of newspapers; photographs of a dozen pretty Englishwomen; a ruler two feet long; a London directory and an almanac.

The erection was finally completed on 12 September 1878. The two sphinxes were added in 1881. For sixty years Cleopatra's Needle has been a world famous landmark of London. It survived almost four-thousand years in Egypt. How long will it stand up to the London climate?

April 1938

Blood Money

by Karl Larsen

Out in the little wood, the farmer Soren Jensen and his cottar were felling a tree, when they saw two blue-coated gendarmes come riding down the road. One of these dismounted and nailed up something bright and red on two of the trees. Then they cantered on in the direction of the town, their uniforms glittering against the white snow in the fields.

As soon as the blue-coats were well out of sight, the two peasants hurried over to see what it was they had posted. It was a placard. Jensen read. "It's about Hans Peersen," he said. He's escaped from jail, and now they're offering us a hundred crowns reward if we catch him."

The cottar looked about as if Peersen might be concealed somewhere near them. "What's that?" he asked. "Well, read it for yourself." But the cottar didn't seem to care particularly about that. They went back to their tree, and continued to discuss Peersen and the posters while they worked. "I wouldn't care to earn *that* hundred crowns," Jensen vowed. The cottar agreed to that readily enough, for there was no doubt that the fugitive could take care of himself.

"Well, I don't know about that. This cold weather has been enough to take the fight pretty well out of him in two days. Still, it would be an ugly way to earn money for he was a fine young fellow, Hans was, when he worked for me." "Well, someone will have to catch him," said Jensen. "That's so. He can't hold out much longer in this weather," the other agreed.

When the farmer came home, he told his wife what he had read on the placards out in the woods. "Lord save us." she cried, and jumped up in alarm. "He won't hurt us any," said Jensen. His wife replied: "I'm not so sure. He's most likely got bad since he's been in prison."

"Hans Peersen was a decent lad when he worked for us," said the farmer, "but everyone treated him like a dog. And that Swedish guard whose throat he cut tormented him early and late." The good wife was alarmed all the same, and started to leave the room. "Don't say a word about this to those silly girls, or to the men either. I told the cottar to keep his mouth shut."

Toward evening the dog in the yard suddenly began to bark, but a voice spoke to it in the darkness, and the uproar ceased at once. The farmer's wife started up. "It's terrible how nervous you are," Jensen said, as he took a lantern and went out. In the middle of the yard stood a man with the dog beside him. "Good evening, master," he said, and you could hear from the quaver in his voice how he shook with cold. It was Hans Peersen. Jensen started and almost dropped the lantern when he saw how miserable the lad looked. "Lord, is that you, Hans!" he said. "I won't hurt you, master."

"No. But I guess it'll be best if I don't seem to know you at all, Hans," said the farmer. "I can't get food any more," the other said simply. Soren Jensen make a quick decision. He turned and went back into the living-room, where his wife stood, almost out of her senses. "Now don't you say a word about all this, Bertha, do you understand?" he said sharply, when he saw that she was ready to scream with fright. "It's nobody's business, and there's nothing to be afraid of."

He went out, and the wife saw his lantern move toward the empty wing of the house where the help ate during harvest time. In a short time the farmer returned and rummaged around alone in the kitchen; then she saw the lantern move toward the wing again, and disappear. Inside the deserted room sat the two men. The gleam from the lantern cast a fitful light over a part of the table. Hans Peersen was greedily eating dry bread and salt meat without a word. "Why don't you put a little lard on the bread?" Jensen asked. But Hans just ate. A long time passed while neither spoke, but when Hans was draining the last drop from the brandy bottle, Jensen said: "Your health."

"Thanks for that, master," the fugitive responded. "And thanks for everything else, too." "We got along well together, didn't we, Hans?" "It was the only place I did get along, master." "I suppose it was." They were silent a moment. "Now you must crawl up into the straw, Hans, and in the morning get away through the hatch before it begins to get light. Good night." Hans looked up quickly. "I'd like to talk with you for a minute," he said.

"What about?" The prisoner looked the farmer in the face. "I can't manage any longer," he said. "No, I don't suppose you can." "They've been down in Ellerup, the police. I saw them nail a placard on a tree, and I wasn't any further away from them than I am from you right now."

"Yes, they've been nailing up those placards around here too." "Has the master seen them, then?" Soren Jensen nodded slowly. "About all the money they offer for me?" "Yes, Hans, I have." "That's a lot of money." Jensen said nothing. "It would be easy enough to earn it," the other continued.

"Yes, Hans, it would, if you don't give yourself up." There was a short pause. "Wouldn't master like to earn that money?" Hans asked at last. The farmer looked at the lad for a long time. "It would be such an easy matter," Hans repeated. Jensen stood up abruptly. "Get up in the straw now, Hans. And see to it that you get away early; before it gets light, so that I don't get into trouble. I might easily, you know."

"Yes; but doesn't master want to earn that money?" "No, I don't want to," the farmer said shortly. "I remember I heard master talking about a little carriage, one like Anders Jensen's. A hundred crowns would come in handy, you know. And then it might be kind of; kind of a little remembrance of me, as you might say. Because they're going to catch me anyway, you know," he added, and continued to look hard at the farmer.

"Well, then it'll go hard with you, Hans." "I know that, master, if nothing happens. But I thought, master has always been so good to me." Soren Jensen was silent. "Won't master drive me in tomorrow then?" "All right, Hans, if it must be, then I'll drive you in."

Next morning everyone on the farm knew that Soren Jensen had captured the murderer, Hans Peersen, just out on the road. He had been so weakened by hunger and cold that he couldn't defend himself at all.

The cart was hitched up. "But I don't want any staring or gaping when we drive off," Jensen had announced. "I don't want to see so much as a cat in the yard." Jensen himself brought breakfast over to the prisoner in the empty wing where he had slept during the night. Everybody watched them from within the rooms, though keeping away from the windows; they saw how the farmer and the prisoner came out together, got into the cart, and drove off.

Hans Peersen was wearing Soren Jensen's own sheepskin coat. Jensen had borrowed another from a neighbour. Neither of them spoke as they drove along the snow-covered country road. Only once Soren said: "It's a dark and toilsome road I'm driving you, Hans." And Hans answered simply: "Let's not talk about it, master."

Finally they came to the market town and drove up to the court house. A pair of indifferent eyes stared out at them from behind a window pane. Just then a young man with gold braid on his cap and a portfolio of papers under his arm came hurrying down the steps of the house across the way. The farmer and his prisoner climbed down from the cart, and Jensen tipped his hat to the young man.

"If you please," he said, "I have brought Hans Peersen." "Hans Peersen? Peersen!" In a twinkling the young man leaped up the stone steps of the court house and cried: "We've caught him. The murderer. The murderer!"

A door was flung hastily open, and two officials came out into the hall. "He's nothing but a young whipper-snapper," said Jensen to Hans. Hans said nothing. But the young man with the gold braided cap was dumbfounded when he saw the farmer shake hands with the murderer.

"Goodbye, master, and thanks," said Hans. "Thanks yourself, Hans," said the other. Hans Peersen mounted the stone steps to the court house. Soren Jensen stood and watched him disappear within.

June 1938

Exchange of Notes

by Sydney Jacobson & Douglas Curtis

Someone sent us a manuscript. We read and liked it, but for various reasons we decided against publishing it in *Lilliput*. So the manuscript was sent back to our contributor with our Chinese rejection slip, which reads like this:

Dear Sir,

If we were a Chinese magazine, we would send back your interesting contribution with this letter, written to a would-be contributor by the editor of a Chinese paper :—

"Illustrious Brother of the Son and Moon. Behold thy servant prostrate before thy feet! I kow-tow to thee, and beg of thy graciousness that thou mayest grant that I may speak and live. Thine honoured manuscript has deigned to cast the light of its august countenance upon me. With raptures I have perused it. By the bones of mine ancestors! Never have I encountered such wit, such pathos, such lofty thought."

"With fear and trembling I return the writing. Were I to publish the treasure thou hast sent me, the Powers would order that it be made a standard of excellence, and that none be published except such that equalled it. Knowing literature as I do, and that it would be impossible in twice ten thousand years to equal what thou hast done, I send back thy writing by guarded servants.

Ten thousand times I crave thy pardon. Behold! My head is at thy feet and I am but dust.

Thy servant's servant,

Wang Chin, Editor."

But as we are not in the land where courtesy goes so far, we need only say: We regret that we are unable to use your contribution in our magazine.

A few days later, we got this reply from our contributor:

Most Excellent Editor, My Honoured Wang Chin. Never before in my slightly distinguished literary career have I received with equal joy and satisfaction the return of my wit, my pathos and my lofty thought. Arise from thy prostration at my feet. All enmity is buried. The fog of our Difference is dispelled by the beams of your Graciousness. By the dust of all our ancestors! It were a merry note withal.

Thy head is no longer at my feet, though I must admit it rolled upon my carpet of finest loom of Samarkand when thy servants presented thy greetings at my morning chop chop. Nor did I spit upon thy wise head, applying as a baser slave might well have done, in pique, my scissors to thy pigtail, my Wang Chin. I place thy head upon my noblest salver and, draping it with my most excellent manuscript (and what more precious wrapping can we conjecture for so sublime a head?) I return it to thee, Wang Chin, my friend, by those same guarded servants who bore it hence, having filled their bellies with rice and savoury frogs from my own tables.

So deeply am I touched about the heart by thy divine communication that I shall make haste to copy for thy *Lilliput* some few dull verses from our father Confucius, knowing full well that you will return them piecemeal and pell-mell, but, ye gods, with a further rapturous note.

And doubtless we may yet seek to force thy hand (a hand beautiful as the tendons of a lily flower) with further literature of gems surpassing the output of a million years. The receipt of thy honourable head will you acknowledge, for I tremble till assured that it is safe upon thy shoulders. Perceive, Wang Chin, I am less than the dust. I grovel and I writhe.

Chin chin. Chu chow. Chop chop.

Thy servant's servant's servant

Douglas Curtis (St.John's Vicarage, Burnley)

August 1938

Clementina's Future

by John Brophy

Although Rudolph and Phedra Phipps lived together in Bloomsbury, they were quite legally and respectably married. Sometimes they had an attack of conscience and felt that their one child, Clementina, would be severely handicapped in her future career by legitimacy. But, as Rudolph always argued, genius could overcome all obstacles. And that Clementina would grow up into a genius could not be doubted, for heredity determined everything, and was not her father a composer of ballets which had been staged in Paris and Stockholm, as well as in London and New York; and were not her mother's novels and treatises upon the theory of art translated into three languages?

The only question which agitated them was: What specific form would Clementina's powers choose for their mature manifestation. In 1922, when Clementina was twelve and in her first year at boarding school - a good school, modern of course - her interests, apart from toffee, seemed to lie in vigorous but uncertain pencil caricatures of her mistresses, and Rudolph and Phedra wondered if she would found a new school of painting, something to mark an epoch, like Vorticism. But later she developed a passion for hockey, her ankles thickened, and her parents were quite downcast. They consulted one of their many psychoanalyst friends, but he said it was only a passing phase.

When Clementina reached the Fifth Form (she never got beyond it) she began to write passionate, but unposted, love letters to the Latin mistress, and Phedra was persuaded that her daughter would become a latter-day and feminine Stendhal. But once she had left school the Latin mistress was quickly forgotten. Clementina decided that she would not go to any university, and Rudolph and Phedra were relieved, not only because there would have been the difficulty of passing the entrance examination, but because money was tight. Sad to relate, Rudolph's ballet music was no longer in demand, and Phedra found increasing difficulty in obtaining a new publisher for her yearly novel. It always had to be a new publisher, after the last book had failed to earn its advance.

They were puzzled to account for this waning of their earning power. In the decade which followed the war they had both been, in their way, quite famous. Not 'popular,' of course. They would have hated that. But quite a nice lot of money had come in to augment their small private income, they had been asked out a lot, their names and often their photographs had appeared frequently in the right sort of journals. And now it was all fading away. The intellectuals were showing a most unintellectual fickleness.

It was all very sad and disillusioning, and they had seriously to consider the prospect of moving to a smaller flat, where there would scarcely be room for their unvarnished bookshelves, their negro sculptures and Siberian carpets, and where their chromium and ebony furniture would look mockingly out of place.

It was at this time that Clementina began to write poetry. Phedra or Rudolph, or perhaps both of them together, would come across her curled up on a divan, a pad on her knees, a pencil bitten between her large, healthy teeth, and her eyes shining with rapture. And proudly they would tiptoe out of the room and tell each other that at last Clementina's genius was finding its proper manifestation.

They never asked to read the poems. They were parents of the modern school, and would not have dreamed of interfering with their child's private life. In her own good time Clementina would show her hand. She did. One morning she came to Phedra and said: "I have had a poem accepted and printed." And she passed over a magazine, the name of which Phedra knew, though a copy had never been admitted to the flat before. It was full of stories of princesses and film stars and gold prospectors, lushly illustrated, and it carried an immense amount of advertising. On the page opened for her inspection Phedra read 'Take Courage: A Poem by Clementina Phipps.' It was awful, it was disastrous, it was emotional, it was lowbrow, it was tripe. And, Clementina had set the name of Phipps to it.

Phedra behaved very well. She simply said: "I'm sure you're proud of it," and went off to tell her husband the worst. By this time, such was the state of their finances, they could not afford to consult a psychoanalyst, but Rudolph looked up his Freud and Jung and Adler, and succeeded in convincing himself that this phase too would pass.

And it was true that never again did they see Clementina with a pad and a pencil. They could not know that with the high fees she was earning she had bought a typewriter and rented a small office in Chancery Lane; that her work was syndicated throughout the British Empire and the United States. Neither Rudolph nor Phedra ever saw the kind of magazines in which it appeared, and for some months they lived in the delusion that that first poem was an aberration, a delusion the happiness of which was only complicated by the increasing difficulty of stretching out an ever-diminishing income to cover a style of living designed in more prosperous times.

Phedra's awakening came when at a party she found herself being introduced as " the mother of Clementina Phipps, you know," and was shown a copy of *The Home Girl's Magazine* with her daughter's name displayed large on the cover and inside a poem.

Phedra went home in tears, to find Rudolph brooding over a piece of wood, designed to be hung as a wall ornament. He said he had seen it in a shop window in Regent Street. There were lots of them, he said, all signed Clementina Phipps. This was no worse than the others, simply a typical specimen. The poem was inscribed in a brown script, burned in with a poker.

Phedra and Rudolph were defeated. They still keep their Bloomsbury flat, for Clementina (who has a house in Mayfair and a villa on the Riviera) makes them a generous allowance. But if you're tactful when you call on them you will assume that they are one of those childless modern couples.

September 1938

The Birth of a Thief

by James Makepeace

HECTOR was a thief, but after a time he reformed. He became a businessman and failed to notice much difference except that the police were respectful now. He did so well that he got married, and was very happy.

But he worried when Muriel, his wife, one day confessed that she in her time had also been a thief. Hector owned up, too, and they decided to let bygones be bygones.

When Muriel announced she was going to have a baby, however, they were very bothered indeed. They had become intensely respectable, but was it not all too probable that their child would inherit thieving tendencies, if not from one parent, then from the other?

And, sure enough, when the boy was born his right list was clenched and nothing would persuade it to open. Hector and Muriel spoke to the doctor, but he said there was no physical defect. He advised them to consult a psychologist.

The psychologist declared he could do nothing about the baby's closed fist unless Hector and Muriel told him the whole story of their lives. So they made him take an oath of secrecy, and then both confessed that they had been thieves.

"Ah," said the psychologist, "now I understand." He took out his gold watch and dangled it in front of the baby's eyes.

And then, slowly, the baby raised his fist, which had never been opened since he was born. Then he made a grab at the watch. The fingers unclenched - and out fell the midwife's ring.

September 1938

"We hear you have some rather original ideas for a coming offensive"

April 1941

Five Missing Flags

by Carl Sagunt

When Archie Barrington, special correspondent to a London daily, entered his club in search of a friendly chat, the first thing he saw was the sulky face of Detective-Inspector McNab of Scotland Yard brooding over a small piece of paper. So intense was the detective that he did not even stir when Barrington stood at his elbow, peering at a photograph which lay on the table in front of him. What he saw was a beautiful girl in a daring bathing dress at the side of a good-looking man of about thirty in shirt sleeves and flannels. Both looked happy.

"The former Miss McNab and her young man on their honeymoon trip, I suppose?" said Barrington. McNab swung round with an angry grunt. "Honeymoon my eye!" he said. "Oh, it's you, Archie. What are you doing in London? "

Archie examined the photograph. "Why are all the really beautiful girls always where I am not?" he sighed. "Who is she, McNab? One of the grateful victims of crime you saved from being kidnapped, I suppose."

"Oh, stop talking nonsense Archie." the Inspector interrupted. "I've never set eyes on that girl. It's the man I'm after. Of all the impudent scoundrels. Breaks out from jail and has the cheek to send me his photo, complete with handwriting and fingerprints."

"Stupid, I call it," Archie said. "After this you can't fail to catch him again."

"Oh, of course, you would, wouldn't you? But the men we have to deal with are cleverer than the readers of your newspaper stories. Well, go and catch the man. Besides all the fun, you can earn five-hundred pounds reward. Just have a look at the back of the photo."

Archie did so. There were only a few words written on it. They ran: "With compliments to my dear friend, Inspector McNab, from C. R. Rowlinson"

"What" he cried. "Is this nice-looking chap the master-thief of Europe? The man who did the pearl-necklace robbery at the Opera House?"

"That's him, blast him!"

"What an ass he is to give himself away just for the pleasure of teasing you!"

"But he did not give himself away! That's what's so infuriating. This photo has been scrutinised by all the experts at the Yard, and they haven't been able to find a single trace to go on. Lots of evidence as to the identity of the sender of course. That's his face all right. No doubt about the handwriting either. These are his fingerprints; we know them rather well at the Yard. Nothing else."

"Any postmark?"

"The photo was posted three days ago at 7 pm in a pillar-box in the West End by one of his gang, I suppose."

"Oh, I see! But all the same, there must be something in the photo to go on. If you can't find it with your x-rays, maybe it can be found with the naked eye. It may be in the picture itself." "You just try, young fellow," the Inspector said, tossing the photograph over the table. "If you think you've got more brains than all the best men of the Yard put together, look at it as long as you like. But please don't tell me that there was a ship's name written on that lifebelt between the two of them, and that it was carefully erased. Even blind hens couldn't help noticing that."

Archie laid the photograph on the table in front of him. The man and the girl in it were standing on what Barrington saw was part of a ship's bridge. There was a wooden partition, with a brass tail on top of it. On the wall, between the two people, an ordinary lifebelt was hanging, but the ship's name and port had been carefully erased. Nothing else was to be seen but a kind of open cupboard, with three rows of pigeon holes, fastened to the wall. Such a picture could have been taken on board almost any steamer.

Suddenly Archie said: "Will you lend me your magnifying glass for a moment, please?"

McNab produced that most important object from his waistcoat pocket. "Not much use in magnifying nothing" he said. "It simply refuses to turn into something even under the most powerful lens."

Archie took the glass and scrutinised minutely a spot on the photograph. Then he took out his notebook and put down some figures.

"Found a clue already?" asked the Inspector. "I knew he was giving himself away with that photo! He overlooked the pigeon holes in the cupboard and so did you."

"No, I didn't. What about them?"

"Five of them are empty!"

"What if they are? What is the cupboard for?"

"Don't you know? They keep the signal flags in it. Five are missing!" And as the inspector stared at him blankly: "Now go and tell the boys at the Yard to get that cheque ready. I hope it will take less than an hour before I can tell you where to find your man!"

But it was not until three hours later that Barrington entered the Inspector's office. "Very sorry to keep you waiting and all that, old chap," he said cheerfully, "but you'll get your man all right. Send a wire to the Port Said police to take him from the Japanese steamer *Nagasaki Maru* due there tomorrow afternoon." Inspector McNab sat back in his chair, open-mouthed.

"He sailed on the 17th of this month from Rotterdam," Archie continued. "The photo was taken on the forenoon of the 24th, and posted in the afternoon of the same day at Marseilles. Give word to the chaps at

Port Said, and they'll collar Rowlinson all right."

McNab regained his speech."Well, if you can prove that."

"Of course I can! After I'd discovered that five flags were missing from the cupboard it was easy. There is one flag for every letter of the A B C, you know. When I examined the cupboard through your magnifying lens I found that in some of the pigeon holes the flags were missing. Five altogether. That gave me an idea. I jotted down the position of the empty pigeon holes in the cupboard, and went to see a friend of mine who is a retired merchant service skipper. He told me at once which were the letters corresponding to the missing flags. Here they are: G-M-O-S-Q."

"Makes very little sense to me," said the Inspector, impatiently.

"Wait a minute. Lots of sense in it, I assure you. In the merchant marine no signal consists of more than four flags. Here I had five. But one of them was the yellow one, corresponding to the letter Q which stands for quarantine, and is hoisted whenever a ship enters port, to warn visitors not to come aboard before the health officials have finished. As the flag Q was in use while the photo was being taken, it's obvious that it was taken at a time when the ship was entering a port."

"Well, if so, the four remaining flags must have formed the signal for the ship's name, which is always hoisted at the same time as the quarantine flag. This signal was composed of the letters G-M-O-S. The next thing to do was to solve a puzzle. I went to a reference library and asked for the International Signal Book, where you find the names of all the ships of the world with the four letters of their signals added to them. From it I extracted the names of all the ships whose signals were composed of the letters G-M-O-S."

"There must have been quite a number!" the Inspector suggested.

"Twenty-four, to be exact. And the name of the ship on which the photo of Rowlinson and the young lady was taken had to be among those twenty-four. It was all a matter of perseverance; and *Lloyds Register*. It tells you practically everything worth knowing about every ship in the world. And then I did some obvious elimination. While checking the names many of them dropped out at once. Rowlinson couldn't possibly be found on a Danish cable ship, or a Soviet ice-breaker. There were the names of four petrol tankers; he couldn't possibly have boarded one of those. Finally the number of the ships on which he might be found boiled down to eight."

"Then I went over the time schedules of those eight steamers. Rowlinson could not be on a ship en route for England from Cape Town or New York. Neither could he possibly be on a boat which is now on mid-ocean between England and Mexico, for that ship only calls at Vera Cruz, so he wouldn't have been able to send the photo in time. Finally there were only two steamers left: the *City of Aberdeen* and the *Nagasaki Maru*. Both had left Europe at the time Rowiinson made his escape. Both had called at a port in time to send the photo. The *Nagasaki Maru* called at Marseilles on the 24th; the *City of Aberdeen* was due at Gibraltar on the 25th.

"I did not think Rowlinson would have boarded the *City of Aberdeen*; he would feel much safer on a non-British ship. But I wanted to make sure, and so I searched for the weather reports for the two ports on the days in question. Well, it rained in torrents at Gibraltar on the 25th, while the weather was fine and warm at Marseilles on the 24th. And the beautiful young lady in the photo is wearing a bathing dress and Rowlinson is in his shirt sleeves. That settled the question."

September 1938

The Lady and The Bear

by Sidonie-Gabrielle Colette

Some fifty years or so ago, an old lady lived on a tract of forest land amid whose ancient trees wolves and bears still roamed. One day her gardener caught a wounded bear, which the old lady took into her house to heal. Under her kind treatment the bear became so tame that he would follow at heel, just like a dog, and sleep peacefully on the sitting-room rug.

One day, when the old lady was walking along a forest path leading to one of the lower farms on the estate, she noticed that Micha, the bear, was following: "No, Micha," she said to the bear, "you are not going to the farm. Go right back home." But Micha refused to go home. So the old lady was obliged to coax him back and lock him up.

Back in the forest, hearing once again a muffled tread on the pine needles, the old lady turned around and saw Micha following her once more. "Oh, Micha," cried the old lady, "I told you not to follow me. You must have jumped out of the window. I'm very angry with you. Go right back home. Go on, now."

And she emphasised her words by two little strokes with her parasol, one, two, across Micha's muzzle. The bear looked at the old lady with a questioning eye, dodged to one side of the path and disappeared swiftly into the forest.

"Now I've done it," the old lady said to herself. "Micha will never want to live with me any more. He's angry. Now he'll run about frightening the sheep and chasing the cattle. I'll go back home and have someone go and look for him."

She retraced her steps, opened the sitting-room door, and found Micha, who hadn't stirred, quietly sleeping on the rug!

The animal in the woods was another bear chasing the old lady to kill and eat her, but, punished by two little strokes with a parasol, and reprimanded like a harmless little poodle, he said to himself: "That high-handed old woman certainly has a kind of power as mysterious as it is unbounded. I'd best take to my heels and be off."

November 1938

January 1946

"Hard cheese, Maisy—your horse wasn't placed"

June 1946

" It's terrible when you think what they grow into. "

Co-Education

by John Brophy

*A note sent from Stall C7 to Stall B23 in the Olympic Theatre, London,
between Act I and Act II, and delivered discreetly by a programme-seller
who had duly been tipped.*

Forgive me if I am dropping a large-size brick, but I have got it firmly
into my head that you are the Eleanor Heald who was one of the first
batch of hapless boys and girls old Trumpington tried his co-educational
theories on at Flenley School.

If my guess is correct (and I'm sure it must be, for you haven't changed
a bit) perhaps you may remember an unprepossessing youngster in your
form, name of Matthewman, who was always getting into trouble because
he was so much in love with you he couldn't attend to his lessons? You
may even remember old Trumps throwing a book at my head because
I would look at your charming face instead of his. For I am that same
Philip Matthewman, older and plumper, worse luck. We haven't met
since we left school and I'd be most grateful if you would spare me a
word at the next interval.

Yours sincerely

P.S. - If by any chance, I have made a ghastly mistake, please accept
my profound apologies. But in that case, may I assure you that you are
the precise double of the most beautiful woman I ever met in my life.

*Note sent from Stall B23 to Stall C7 between Act II and III and delivered
by the same programme-seller.*

Dear Philip; You are just as romantic and flattering as ever. From the brief
glimpse I've had of you I wouldn't say you were very much plumper, but
I doubt if you've grown up at all. Perhaps that book old Trumps threw
at you permanently arrested your mental development? Anyhow, it was
very nice of you to recognise me after all these years.

I think it would only spoil our little reunion if you came across now
and we had to talk in front of these people I'm with. They're quite nice,
really, but if they knew I was writing a note in the cloakroom to a man in
the audience, their eyes would pop out. You seem to be alone. Could you
wait after the show? I'll push my friends into a taxi, and then you can see
me home. By the way, I'm now Mrs Charles Rood.

Yours truly

P.S. - This is like old school days. Do you remember how we passed notes to each other then?

Final Note passed between Stall C7 and Stall B23 by an amused but thrice-tipped programme-seller.

I should say I do remember. But you've forgotten that old Trumps was always a rotten throw, and the book missed me. So my retarded development can't be blamed on that. Of course I'll be waiting. As long as you like.

Letter from Kasrel Nil, Malvern to 73 Auriol Square, London.

My Dear Eleanor; Will you ever forgive me for making that stupid gaffe about your husband? You see, I feel I know you so well, so intimately, and yet I'm blankly ignorant of all that's happened to you since we were at school. Fortunately, if I may so put it, your bereavement is not recent, so I hope my clumsiness didn't hurt you too keenly. Another thing I feel I must apologise for is a little difficult to explain. I mean, the way I kept referring to the old days at school. It has just occurred to me it may have been embarrassing to you.

I fully realise I was a most objectionable boy. I can't in honesty blame myself for falling in love with you; that was inevitable. But the way I would sit and stare, most of the time with my mouth wide open, I dare say, must have been ludicrous when it wasn't exasperating. No wonder old Trumps lost his temper with me. It's a wonder you didn't do the same. But you were always sweet and charitable, as friendly and cool as you are today, never giving me the slightest encouragement and yet never snubbing me out of hand.

I can't begin to tell you how much I enjoyed going around with you. You transformed an old bachelor's periodic visit to Town, a matter of dull routine, into an exquisite adventure. And, by the way, I find I shall have to be in Town again much sooner than I expected. If you have next Thursday, Friday and Saturday free, could you and would you keep them for me?

Yours sincerely

Letter from 73 Auriol Square to Kasrel Nil

My dear Philip; Not so much of the old bachelor. You must remember we're the same age to within a month or two, and if you talk about yourself as if you were in a decline, you're being rude to me. And you'd never be that, would you, my dear, polite, chivalrous, romantic and rather stupid friend?

No, you can't have Thursday, Friday and Saturday. I've never heard of such a thing. You'll be getting me talked about, the way you did at school. You'll notice that, unlike you, I'm quite shameless and don't mind talking about those days a bit. And, for your private ear, though you mustn't let it make you conceited, you weren't at all the sort of boy you seem to imagine you were. Far from it. Of course I laughed at you. I still do. But in all friendliness, Philip, I don't think anyone could help being fond of you.

Friday I'm booked, and I won't attempt to call it off. Telephone me when you arrive.

Yours truly

Letter from 73 Auriol Square to Kasrel Nil

Philip, it was sweet of you to send those flowers, after you'd left to catch your train. Carnations, too. But what a queer, uninquisitive creature you are. You know I've got a daughter, and yet you never ask a single question about her. If I didn't know you so well, I'd think you were jealous. But I suppose it's just your idea of being discreet and not putting your nose into other people's business.

My dear Philip, I'm as proud as a peacock about the child, though I take care not to let her know it. She's fifteen now, and she'll be taking Matric in the summer. Only they don't call it Matric now, but some high-falutin' name I forget. I'm sending you a photograph of Eleanor, she's got the same name as me, in this letter. People say she's very like what I was at her age. Though, of course, she's got no pigtail. A very good thing, too. I'm all in favour of short hair. Do you remember the time Jimmy Durrant pulled my pigtail, and you blacked his eye for him?

Yours reminiscently

Extract from a very long letter from Kasrel Nil, to 73 Auriol Square.

. . . The photograph of your daughter quite upset me. Please don't think I'm rude, or that I shan't love the child. But she is so like you when you were at school, that it all came back to me. . . . I understand very well your feeling of responsibility towards her, for I am the sole guardian of a young nephew of the same age. My brother and his wife are both in India and, funnily enough, young Philip, they called him after me, is at Flenley School. By all his accounts, old Trumpington is still the same sentimental kindly, dear old gasbag as ever. . . .

A postcard from 73 Auriol Square, to Kasrel Nil.

How very queer! My daughter is also at Flenley. Surely she can't be in the same form as your Philip? Anyhow, I'm going down on Saturday to see her, and I'll find out and let you know.

Telegram from Malvern Post Office to 73 Auriol Square.

Will meet you Flenley Station two-thirty today, Philip.

Note from Master Philip Matthewman to Miss Eleanor Rood, left in a secret hiding place behind the parallel bars in the Flenley school gymnasium.

I could have dropped down dead when Uncle Philip walked in with your mother. Of course, I didn't know she was your mother then. I couldn't make out what they started to laugh about. When you'd gone back to your desk, and old Trumps called me out, Uncle P gave me one look and said, "Where did you get that bruise on your cheek?" Naturally, I wasn't going to spill the beans, but old Trumps, true to his preaching, evidently felt he had to come clean, so he clears his throat and says, "I'm afraid, Mr. Matthewman, that is my fault. The fact is I lost my temper with the boy and threw a book at him."

I was scared stiff the old josser would let on about my looking at you instead of at the blackboard, but he only muttered something about, "Far too young, far too young! The very sort of thing co-education is designed to prevent." And, fortunately, neither Uncle P nor your mother seemed to be paying any attention. Instead, they went into a fit of rather disgusting hysterical laughter, as you saw. And what my uncle said to old Trumps when they were going away, was, "Congratulations, sir. Your aim has improved." Funny thing to say, wasn't it? See you later.

P.S. - I wonder if my uncle and your mother met on the train coming down? I'd no idea theyeven knew each other.

Fragment from a note left in the same hiding place by Miss Eleanor Rood

. . . You're the complete bughouse for sheer purblind stupidity. Couldn't you see Holy Matrimony written all over them? Bet you a strawberry ice it's announced in *The Times* before the end of term.

Item from Tuck Shop debited against Master P. Matthewman

Two (2) Strawberry Ices . . . .8d.

January 1939

What They Say at Breakfast

by Antonia White

Three Years: Want bacon. Don't want porridge. Nasty porridge. Milly's not a baby. Milly wants bacon.

Seven Years: Why must I have milk, Mummy? Well, horses are strong, aren't they? Horses don't drink milk after they've stopped being babies, do they? Why don't you scold Lulu? She hasn't drunk her milk and she's much littler than me? Can I have a penny if I drink it all up, Mummy?

Twelve Years: You disgusting little beast, Lulu. You've only left me three sausages. Chuck me that hunk of bread; can't wait for more toast. I'm late for Wiggsy as it is. Anyone seen my French grammar? No, really, Mums, my neck's quite clean. It's just the light. Can I have tuppence, Mums, please, to buy a bar of chocolate on the way to school? Otherwise I'll be faint by lunch time!

Fifteen Years: I can't help being late. It takes years to fix my hair this way. Well, I like it, anyway. So does Rosalind. There's no need to keep all this mass of food for me. I only want some grapefruit and black coffee. And why shouldn't I slim if I want to. Cheeky? Mother, why am I too young to use lipstick? Rosalind does, and she's three weeks younger than me.

Eighteen Years: Are you absolutely sure there isn't a letter for me? Lulu, are you positive no one 'phoned for me last night? Everyone in this house is so awful about taking messages. No, no one in particular. I just wondered, that's all. No, I don't want any breakfast, thanks. I think I'll go for a walk. No, I'm not going by the fishmonger's, Mother. Where? Oh, nowhere in particular. Anywhere where I can be alone.

Twenty-Two Years: Oh, darling, even having breakfast with you is exciting. When I think of those ghastly family breakfasts; years and years of them. We won't get stodgy and awful like that ever, will we? Sweetheart, why do you have to rush off to a beastly office? Nine whole hours before I see you again. I don't know how I'm going to bear it.

Twenty-Four Years: Dick do hurry. You've missed the 9.05 twice this week already. Just suppose you lost your job now – of all times! You needn't hurry back if you want to put in a bit of overtime. I'm going over to Mother's tonight. She's going to give me some marvellous patterns of things Lulu and I had when we were babies. I'll leave you something in the fridge. I just can't face cooking these days. Now, run along, there's a good boy.

Thirty Years: Sally, dear, don't mess up your egg like that, you're a big girl now. Come along, Jackie, drink up your milk. I'm sure Mummy never made a fuss about drinking up her milk. Dick, dear, if you left five minutes earlier this morning, you'd have time to call in at the greengrocer and tell him to send six oranges before lunch. I need them for baby's orange juice. And you won't forget to leave me that cheque for the butcher, will you?

Forty Years: I don't care what your father says. You'll go straight upstairs and wash that stuff off your face before you have your breakfast. You're far too young to use make-up. I don't know what girls are coming to these days. Richard, that's not true! And, even if it were, it's wicked of you to try and undermine my authority with the children. It's outrageous, the way you spoil Sally. Oh, darling, do you really think I was prettier at her age?

Forty-Five Years: Oh, Richard, how could you? And I've always trusted you implicitly. It wasn't my fault. May put the letter in the pile by my plate and I opened it without even looking at the address. Thank goodness the children are all away from home. But they'll have to know when the divorce begins. No, Richard, there's no other way out. It's all over for us. How can you think, after this, that . .?

Fifty Years: Sir Richard. Doesn't it sound splendid? Of course, now you're going to be knighted, darling, I'll need some really nice new clothes. You don't want your old wife to be a disgrace to you, do you?

Sixty Years: Just grapefruit and black coffee, please, Simmonds. And why shouldn't I slim at my age, if I want to? Just because I am a grandmother, there's no need to look like one, is there? Sixty's no age at all these days.

Seventy Years: Sally, dear, I do hope you're not seriously contemplating divorce. We've never had such a thing in our family. Your father would turn in his grave at the thought. You know, dear, I've lived a long time and I can't help feeling it's always a wife's fault if her husband is unfaithful. When I think of my Richard; never the least shadow of trouble between us.

Eighty Years: I want some bacon. Bacon, do you hear? I'm sick of this horrible porridge. Only fit for babies. I don't care if it is bad for me. I WANT BACON.

August 1939

Black Money

by Edward Stevenson

Ludwig Braun's ruddy face turned sallow. His round fat figure half arose from his chair, as if he were about to obey his wild desire to flee. But he knew that that would be the worst sort of folly. It was easier to escape one's conscience than to elude the Gestapo.

He sank back into his chair. After all, this was what one had to expect. The very success of his scheme had been a bad omen. He looked at his trembling clerk. "I will see Herr Walther," he said quietly. Walther was a tall man, with a pocked face. When they had exchanged Heil Hitlers, he said, "I am to inform you that Herr Hoffmann wishes to see you. At once"

Braun's worst fears were realised. Kurt Hoffmann was a power in the Gestapo, because of his intimacy with Der Fuehrer some even rated his influence as greater than Himmler's. He was one of those mysterious men whose functions were ill defined, but whose names struck terror in every heart. His clerks stared after him with frightened eyes as he went out of the office with Walther. It was probably the last time they would see him, Braun reflected.

He and Walther got into the brown limousine that awaited them. It was a fine spring day, but Braun was in no mood to enjoy the beauties of nature. He slumped in a corner and noticed nothing. When he finally aroused himself sufficiently to look out of the window, he was surprised to find that they were speeding through the suburbs. Presently they entered the grounds of a large estate and drove along the winding road that led to the great white mansion, which could be seen through the trees. A butler admitted them.

"Herr Braun," Walther said to the butler. "Herr Braun is expected," the butler said. Walther remained downstairs as the butler escorted Braun to a large sunny room on the second floor. At a wide desk in the centre of the room sat Kurt Hoffmann.

"Will you sit down, Herr Braun?" Hoffmann said. Braun sat down heavily. Across the broad expanse of desk Hoffmann was smiling at him. He was a thin man, with black, disorderly hair, thick spectacles, and a drawn, colourless face. His crooked smile looked as if it had been sewn on his mouth with red thread.

"You are Herr Braun, the exporter?" "Yes, Herr Hoffmann."

"You specialise in toys?" "Yes."

"And dolls?" "Dolls, among other things." " But, lately you have been doing very well with dolls?"

"Business has been good, it is true." With difficulty he controlled an impulse to blurt out the truth. "All right!" he wanted to shout. "Enough of this cat-and-mouse game. Out with it."

"A Monsieur Roget of Paris is a good customer of yours?" They knew everything. "He is one of my customers."

"Your best customer from all reports." He opened a drawer of his desk and produced a large cheap doll. "This model is a great favourite in Paris, I am told." Braun began to perspire. He could feel drops of sweat cooling on his brow. "I have sold many of those."

Hoffmann tore the thin dress from the doll's body, revealing its misshapen nakedness. "Observe, Herr Braun." He took a knife and split the doll's body. "What does one get for marks in Paris today, Herr Braun?" He did not look at Braun; he was busy disembowelling the doll.

"I—I do not know," Braun faltered.

"Do you think I am a fool?"

"I assure you—I"

"Bah. Don't you think I know what you have been up to?" He held up the depleted doll. "Have you ever seen this trick?" From another drawer he produced a stack of paper marks. Crumpling them into tight wads, he stuffed the doll with them. "A great many marks can be smuggled out of the country in fifty thousand dolls, eh?" Braun did not answer.

"Jewels, too, make a fine stuffing, do they not? If one has no faith in the Third Reich, if one fears inflation, one has only to go to Braun the Exporter and he will smuggle one's money and jewels out of the country and have them converted into sterling or dollars, eh, Herr Smuggler?" Braun stared dumbly at his smiling inquisitor.

"Ah, yes!" Hoffmann continued. "Braun the Exporter knows how to dispose of black money. For ten per cent he will see that his clients get complete satisfaction." His sewn smile remained fixed even when he spoke. "You do not seem to have a high regard for your neck, my friend."

"I am not afraid to die," Braun replied simply. It was strange, but suddenly he did not fear death.

Hoffmann leaned forward. "Perhaps you do not have to die," he said. "Perhaps we are more interested in learning the names of your clients, those poor wretches who have so little faith in the glorious destiny of the Third Reich. Some of your clients are quite prominent, I hear."

"I will not buy my life with treachery," Braun said.

"The ethics of treason. But perhaps we might persuade you to talk."

"My lips are sealed."

"Look here, Braun, I will make you an offer. I have reason to suspect that Captain Unger is one of your clients. Expose him and you will go free." "No!"

"One little exposure is a small price to pay for one's life. Come now." "No!"

"Consider, Braun. Your life for Unger's. Are you mad?" "My lips are sealed," Braun said.

"Then I can do nothing for you. You must pay the penalty for your treason on the block."

"I am ready."

Hoffmann's eyes gleamed behind his thick glasses. "I salute your bravery, Herr Braun," he said. "But it so happens that Captain Unger has already told me that he is a client of yours."

Braun tried to conceal his surprise and chagrin. Perhaps Hoffmann was trying to trap him.

"I know no Captain Unger," he said.

Hoffmann arose and extended his hand. "My congratulations, Herr Braun, on your bravery and discretion. You are all that Captain Unger said you were."

Braun took the extended hand and stared blankly at Hoffmann.

"In view of your qualifications," Kurt Hoffmann said, "I shall be pleased to have you handle my export business, too."

September 1939

Just a Mood

by Theodora Benson

First thing that morning when Julian Lasker got to the office they said that he was in one of his moods. Not, as they freely admitted at *Hail and Lasker's* that there was any harm in Mr Lasker. His moods mostly consisted of saying "Good God" a great deal, and of his hair standing on end.

He was chiefly liable to moods when Hail was away, on account of the extra work. Nothing occurred that morning to soothe him any. Typescripts he'd have to read himself mounted up around him. Readers' reports came in with sitting-on-the-fence accounts of novels written with some distinction, which on the one hand might look creditable in the list and on the other hand might not altogether sell largely.

"Look creditable, Good God! What does he think the list is: The Royal Academy? Not sell well, huh? We've all got to eat, haven't we?" Lasker, with his waisted elegance, did not look as though he ate very much. On the other hand he had to drink more than he cared to at lunch to keep one of his best-selling, laziest authors in temper and in countenance. He received the news that the book looked like being yet another three months behind schedule, and a request for a further advance.

Towards six o'clock the girl turned up at the office. *Hail and Lasker* prided themselves on an absence of red tape over receiving people; unless they were already stuck with an interview, anybody could come and bother them any time. Inquiries put a call through to Lasker and he said: "Oh, all right, show her in."

She drifted in on fantastically high heels, she smoked through a long cigarette holder, her hair grew long and was curled at the ends, she was rather long herself. She wore no hat, and she was very smartly dressed, though a little too thinly for the weather. She looked pretty, vague, elegant and effete. At any other time he'd have been liable to like her.

"You Mr Lasker?" He admitted it.

"I've knocked off a first novel," she said, with just a trace, but not more, of apology in her voice. She laid an unwrapped and rather untidy typescript, which had been under her arm, upon his desk. "I want you to read it this weekend," she said.

"Good God!" Julian Lasker's dark curls sprang in all directions "This weekend; Good God! See those piles of stuff? Know who's got to read 'em all? I've got to. That's who, me."

"All right, all righty," said the girl, "don't fret yourself, hon. Maybe you could get round to reading it next month."

Julian's soulful dark eyes filled with frenzy. "Next month's impossible. Next month I'm going on holiday. Good God! I should hope so. Hail's away on holiday. Morden's away on holiday,"

"Who's Morden?" "Morden's a third of us mugs. He's always on holiday. But next month it'll be me."

"All righty, all right," she said. She gave him a friendly glance which any other day would have pleased him. "It doesn't matter. I'm going away myself come to that. I'd rather you just hung on to my stuff yourself till you've got leisure for it. Any time that suits you. Just any time at all." She nodded agreeably, turned to the door, said "So long, Toots," and was gone.

Lasker looked indignantly at the typescript on his desk. Its title was an added exasperation: *Angela Prefers Nuts*. This weekend, indeed, Good God! He turned back the cover and began to read. Dinner was an unwelcome interruption. It wasn't till supper and cabaret that they cajoled him right out of his preoccupation. Even then he was thankful when he could get back to the novel.

It was more than easy reading, it gripped you like glue. Although there was something savage about it, it was not without humanity. In spite of its naive-seeming idiom there was, if you cared to look, something profound. It was relentlessly funny.

Julian arrived at the office next day bleary-eyed but exalted, every hair in place. Here, he thought, was an honest-to-God, first-rate, sure-fire, best-seller, and when he felt as strongly as that he had never been wrong. Whatever his faults, he had flair.

"There's the name and address on the typescript. Get her for me on the telephone." A moment later his secretary said: "They say she's gone away."

"What the - here, give it me." He grabbed it and asked: "When's she expected back?" "She didn't say. We've absolutely no idea, sir." "Where's she gone to?" "Central Asia."

"But she's left a forwarding address?" "Oh no, sir. She said to keep everything till she came back, unless she wrote for it. She said she wasn't expecting anything interesting for a long time."

All over his head his dark curls began to spring slightly from place. "Good God!" said Mr Lasker.

September 1939

"I see no objection to your scrapping those old files—providing you take copies of them!"

July 1946

Midnight Visit

by Robert Arthur

Ausable did not fit any description of a secret agent Fowler had ever read. Following him down the musty corridor of the gloomy French hotel where Ausable had a room, Fowler felt let down. It was a small room, on the sixth and top floor, and scarcely a setting for a figure of romantic adventure. But Ausable, in his wrinkled business suit badly in need of cleaning, could hardly be called a romantic figure.

He was, for one thing, fat. Very fat. And then there was his accent. Though he spoke French and German passably, he had never altogether lost the New England twang he had brought to Paris from Boston more than twenty years before.

"You are disappointed," Ausable said wheezily over his shoulder. "You were told that I was a secret agent, a spy, dealing in espionage and danger. You wished to meet me because you are a writer, young and romantic. You visioned mysterious figures in the night, the crack of pistols, drugs in the wine. Instead, you have spent a dull evening in a French music hall with a sloppy fat man who, instead of having messages slipped into his hand by dark-eyed beauties, gets only a prosaic telephone call making an appointment in his room. You have been bored!"

The fat man chuckled to himself as he unlocked the door of his room and stood aside to let his discomfited guest enter. "You are disillusioned," Ausable told him. "But take cheer, my young friend. Presently you will see a paper, a quite important paper for which several men have risked their lives, come to me in the next-to-the-last step of its journey into official hands. Someday soon that paper may well affect the course of history. In that thought there is drama, is there not?"

As he spoke, Ausable closed the door behind him. Then he switched on the light. And as the light came on, Fowler had his first authentic thrill of the day. For, halfway across the room, a small automatic in his hand, stood a man. Ausable blinked a few times.

"Max," he wheezed, "you gave me a start. I thought you were in Berlin. What are you doing here in my room?" Max was slender, a little less than tall, with features that suggested slightly the crafty pointed countenance of a fox. There was about him, aside from the gun, nothing especially menacing.

"The report," he murmured. "The report that is being brought to you tonight on Germany's air strength. I thought it would be safer in my hands than in yours." Ausable moved to an armchair and sat down heavily. "I'm going to raise hell with the management this time, and you can bet on it," he said grimly. "The second time in a month somebody has gotten into my room off that confounded balcony."

Fowler's eyes went to the single window of the room. It was an ordinary window, against which now the night was pressing blackly. "Balcony?" Max said, with a rising inflection. "No, a passkey. I did not know about the balcony. It might have saved me some trouble if I had."

"It's not my damned balcony," Ausable said with extreme irritation. "It belongs to the next apartment." He glanced explanatorily at Fowler. "You see," he said, "this room used to be part of a large unit, and the next room, through that door there, used to be the living room. It had the balcony, which extends under my window now. You can get onto it from the empty room two doors down and somebody did, last month. The management promised me to block it off. But they haven't."

Max glanced at Fowler, who was standing stiffly a few feet from Ausable, and waved the gun with a little peremptory gesture. "Please sit down," he suggested. "We have a wait of half an hour at least, I think."

"Thirty-one minutes," Ausable said moodily. "The appointment was for twelve-thirty. I wish I knew how you learned about that report, Max." The other smiled without mirth.

"And we wish we knew how it was got out of Germany," he replied. "However, no harm has been done. I will have it back. What is that?" Unconsciously Fowler, who was still standing, had jumped at the sudden rapping on the door. Ausable yawned.

"The gendarmes," he said. "I thought that so important a paper as the one we are waiting for might well be given a little extra protection tonight." Max bit his lip in uncertainty. The rapping was repeated. "What will you do now, Max?" Ausable asked. "If I do not answer, they will enter anyway. The door is unlocked. And they will not hesitate to shoot."

The man's face was black as he backed swiftly toward the window; with his hand behind him he flung it up to its full height, and swung a leg over the sill. "Send them away!" he rasped. "I will wait on the balcony. Send them away or I'll shoot and take my chance!"

The rapping on the door came louder. And a voice was raised. "M'sieu! M'sieu Ausablel." Keeping his body twisted so that his gun still covered the fat man and his guest, the man at the window grasped the frame with his free hand to support himself as he rested his weight on one thigh; then he swiftly swung his other leg up and over the sill.

The doorknob turned. Swiftly Max pushed with his left hand to free himself from the sill and drop to the balcony outside. And then, as he dropped, he screamed once, shrilly. The door opened and a waiter stood there with a tray, a bottle and two glasses.

"M'sieu, the cognac you ordered for when you returned," he said, and set the tray upon the table, deftly uncorked the bottle, and retired.

White-faced, Fowler stared after him. "But," he stammered, police..."

"There were no police." Ausable sighed. "Only Henri, whom I was expecting"

"But won't that man ..." Fowler began.

"No," Ausable said, "he won't return. There is no balcony."

October 1939

A Story From Spain

by Ernest Hemingway

An old man with steel-rimmed spectacles and very dusty clothes sat by the side of the road. There was a pontoon bridge across the river and carts, trucks, men, women and children were crossing it. The mule-drawn carts staggered up the steep bank from the bridge with soldiers helping push against the spokes of the wheels. The trucks ground up and away, heading out of it all, and the peasants plodded along in the ankle deep dust.

But the old man sat there without moving. He was too tired to go any farther. It was my business to cross the bridge, explore the bridgehead beyond and find out to what point the enemy had advanced. I did this and returned over the bridge. The old man was still there.

"Where do you come from?" I asked him. "From San Carlos," he said, and smiled. That was his native town and so it gave him pleasure to mention it, and he smiled. "I was taking care of animals," he explained. "Oh," I said, not quite understanding.

"Yes," he said, "I stayed, you see, taking care of the animals. I was the last one to leave the town of San Carlos." He did not look like a shepherd nor a herdsman, and I looked at his black, dusty clothes and his grey, dusty face and his steel-rimmed spectacles and said, "What animals were they?"

"Various animals," he said. "I had to leave them."

I was watching the bridge and the African looking country of the Ebro Delta and wondering how long now it would be before we would see the enemy, and listening all the while for the first noises that would signal that ever mysterious event called contact, and the old man still sat there.

"What animals were they?" I asked again. "There were three animals altogether," he explained. "There were two goats and a cat and then there were four pairs of pigeons."

"And you had to leave them?" "Yes, because of the artillery. The captain told me to go because of the artillery."

"And you have no family?" I asked, watching the far end of the bridge where a few last carts were hurrying down the bank. "No," he said, "only the animals I stated. The cat, of course, will be all

73

right. A cat can look out for itself, but I cannot think what will become of the others."

"What politics have you?" I asked. "I am without politics," he said. "I am 76 years old. I have come twelve kilometres now and I think I can go no farther."

"This is not a good place to stop," I said. "If you can make it, there are trucks up the road where it forks for Tortosa." "I will wait a while," he said, "and then I will go. Where do the trucks go?" "Towards Barcelona"

"I know of no one in that direction," he said, "but thank you very much."

He looked at me very blankly and tiredly then said, having to share his worry with someone, "The cat will be all right, I am sure. There is no need to be unquiet about the cat. But the others. Now what do you think about the others?"

"Why they'll probably come through it all right." "You think so?"

"Why not?" I said, watching the far bank where now there were no carts.

"But what will they do under the artillery when I was told to leave because of the artillery?"

"Did you leave the dove cage unlocked?" I asked. "Yes."

"Then they'll fly." "Yes, certainly they'll fly. But the others. It's better not to think about the others," he said.

"If you are rested I would go," I urged. "Get up and try now."

"Thank you," he said, and got to his feet, swayed from side to side, and then sat down backwards in the dust. "I was taking care of animals," he said dully, but no longer to me. "I was only taking care of animals."

There was nothing to do about him. The Fascists were advancing toward the Ebro. It was a grey, overcast day with a low ceiling, so their planes were not up. That, and the fact that cats know how to look after themselves, was all the good luck that old man would ever have.

October 1939

How I Won the Iron Cross

by Erwin Blumenfeld

During the last world war, I had the honour of spending part of my youth as a German ambulance driver on the Western front. And there it was I won the Iron Cross. At that time (things are different now) I was still too young to be brave. I was only eighteen.

One day as we were resting peacefully, the Corporal called me:

"Blumenfeld," he said, "you're a brainy fellow, you know French. In a month's time I shall be going on leave, and by then I must know French perfectly. Perfectly, do you understand? If you can teach me perfect French in one month, I'll give you the Iron Cross."

"First or Second Class?" I inquired. At that he became angry, and shouted: "I could order you to teach me French if I wanted to! But you'll obey me even without orders, do you understand?"

"Yes, Corporal." I realised that I shouldn't be able to get anything more in the way of decorations out of him, so I asked whether, in view of the exhausting brain work these lessons would entail, I might stay in bed until nine in the morning. This permission was granted.

The next morning at ten o'clock I reported to the Corporal. I did not possess a French grammar book, but I happened at that time to be reading Stendhal's *Le Rouge Et Le Noir*. I took this book along with me and explained respectfully to the Corporal that the first thing he must do was accustom his tongue and his ear to the sound of French vowels. For this purpose, I told him, he must learn the whole of Stendhal's book by heart.

I read aloud very slowly:"La petite ville de Verrieres peut passer pour l'une des plus jolies de la Franche-Comte." The Corporal repeated this five hundred times. A week later, with a little assistance from me, he was almost word perfect. I then went on to the second sentence: "Ses maisons blanches, avec leurs toits pointus de tuiles."

Inspired Stendhal! This sentence was too much for my Corporal. He shouted, he stuttered, I saw tears in his eyes. He spluttered, he fought, he struggled. But he never succeeded in memorising even the first ten words. A week later I was summoned to the orderly room. "Blumenfeld," said the Corporal, "I've had enough of you and your French lessons. I shan't need you any more." "But what about my Iron Cross?"

"Your Iron Cross? Well, I'm a man of my word. You shall have your Iron Cross." "First Class? With the black and white ribbon?"

"Yes, blast you, with the black and white ribbon. Now get out." I left the room. I was a hero. I had won the Iron Cross.

And nowadays, whenever I look at a photograph of Herr Hitler proudly wearing the Iron Cross on his breast, I think: "I wonder how he won his? I know he can't speak French".

December 1939

The Broadcast

by Henry Cecil

This is the *BBC* Home Service. We must apologise to our listeners for being three days late with the news, but the Ministry of Information notified us that, while we could take it as quite official that nothing whatever had happened, it would be as well not to publish this statement immediately as it might lead to panic.

At the same time the Ministry informed us that if we chose to assume from the statement that nothing whatever had happened that something had possibly happened we should not be altogether wrong, while if we choose to assume that the something in question had reference to an event which took place last Wednesday week, we could assume it if we liked. Subsequently the Ministry cancelled the above instructions and said that in no circumstances was any statement to be made. This cancellation was then cancelled, and we were instructed that in no circumstances must no statement be made.

Shortly afterwards this was changed, and we were told that in no circumstances must any statement not covered by the previous instructions be issued by us. While we were still considering how to comply with these last instructions, we were informed that the Ministry of Information had adopted an entirely new policy, and that all previous instructions must be disregarded.

Before I read the news bulletin here is an announcement. We have just been informed that hostile aircraft are approaching England from the direction of the North Sea. If you will refer to the map printed on page 27 of the current issue of the *Radio Times* you will see that the country is divided into numbered squares. According to the latest information the aircraft are approaching Square Ten. I will repeat that. Hostile aircraft are approaching Square Ten.

While I am waiting for further news of their approach I should remind you of the map of London appearing on page 28 of this week's issue of the *Radio Times*. You will see that this is also divided into numbered squares. Ah! Here is some news. Several squadrons of our fighters have just gone up to meet the enemy. I naturally cannot state the aerodromes from which they have gone up, but those of you who have the *Radio Times* open before you will know where I mean if I say that they have gone up from Squares Three, Six and Nine. The hostile aircraft have now reached Square 15.

I hope I shall be able to see them soon and describe them to you. More British fighters have gone up. Squares Two, Eight and Ten. Anti-aircraft guns are now firing. Squares Three and Six. The enemy have now reached square 16. We should be able to see them soon. It's a lovely day and the streets are crowded. They couldn't have had a better day for it.

George Gimlet has just arrived to help me give you the best picture of this raid. It is a gorgeous day, isn't it, George? Yes-yes-gorgeous-gorgeous.

Do you think it is finer than the day of the daylight raid during the last war? I should say it's about the same.

Anyway, everyone is in fine form and determined to make the most of it. We can just see our aircraft disappearing in the distance. We can distinctly hear the guns. There isn't a cloud in the sky. Everyone is tremendously excited. Ah; there they are. Do you see them George? Oh; no, sorry—they were birds. The guns are getting nearer.

Hullo. That was close. A piece of shrapnel has just fallen in the street outside the room from which we are talking. Square One. Just missed an old lady. She doesn't seem to have minded in the least. A policeman has just told the crowd to keep moving.

Ah, there they really are. Magnificent, aren't they? Each one is like a silver, a silver .. George is better at this than I am. You take over, George.

Good afternoon, everyone. This is George Gimlet. Yes, it's a glorious sight. Not a cloud in the sky except the gentle puffs made by the anti-aircraft gun shells. I cannot do the scene justice. The enemy planes number about 35, would you say 35 or 34? Well 30 to 35. They are going beautifully in formation. I would say they were about over Square 22. Anyone in the neighbourhood of Square 22 should see them perfectly. They have only to look straight up.

The noise is getting louder. Several more pieces of shrapnel have fallen in the street. Ah, that was much louder. I would say that was a bomb, wouldn't you, Charles? Yes, I should say so. I'll find out. Yes, that was a bomb dropped in the Round Pond. Square 21. I will repeat that. A bomb has just been dropped in Square 21.

Hullo. The anti-aircraft guns have stopped firing. Oh. I see; it's our aircraft. Aren't they magnificent? There must be 60 or 70 of them. They are making straight for the enemy. Square 12.

The enemy are turning round. They are obviously going to make a bolt for it. There was another bomb. And that one. And that one. Our planes are going simply magnificently. The other fellows are doing well, too, but we're overtaking them. We're gaining on them. Oh, the last three bombs which were dropped were in Squares Four, Nine and 13.

I say, what a speed, isn't it, Charles? Terrific. They are almost out of sight. I should say over Square 15. Can you see them still? No, they must be nearing the coast now. It has been a magnificent spectacle.

Ah, there go the warning sirens.

January 1940

Shaw and the Amazon

by Odette Keun

George Bernard Shaw recently wrote an article imparting the information that in this war, and in this country, women resembled the females of the Danakil tribe in Abyssinia, who exacted from their suitors, before marriage, four trophies cut off from the bodies of four dead enemies; that anyhow women were always much more bloodthirsty than men; and that democratic England and France were neither better nor more in the right than Nazi Germany. So there.

It was immediately disclosed by trustworthy travellers who had gone to Abyssinia, which Bernard Shaw hasn't, that a Danakil bride contents herself with evidence that her husband has killed a lion or an elephant, a perfectly proper precaution in a community which lives by the chase, and necessary to assure her that he is a sufficiently good hunter to support a family.

Moreover, this precaution has its equivalent in every civilized society. The only difference is that a prospective European husband is required to show that he is able to hunt money successfully, while a Danakil male only needs to show that he is able to hunt animals. So much for Bernard Shaw's first derogatory assertion.

Regarding his second point, that women are more bloodthirsty than men, what argument can he advance except his own opinion? Mine is just as good as his, and I maintain that they aren't. To begin with, in civilised nations the nerves of women are much weaker than men's and normally shrink from the display of blood when it is shed by violence. No woman of a civilised race ever formed a regiment for active killing.

I've lived in countries; Turkey before its modernisation, Russia under the Tsars and under the Communists, the Caucasus, where periodical massacres were the rule, of Armenians, Greeks, Jews, or whatever political group the governments (composed, by the way, of men, not women) happened to want to exterminate. Some of them took place in front of my eyes, and I testify that I never saw, or heard of, women hacking men, women and children to pieces, hanging them by the feet, drowning them tied back to back, roasting them, or burying them head down, alive, in the snow. No. It was members of Bernard Shaw's own sex who played these amiable little jokes.

Nor did women, in any case which I can remember in history, invent judicial systems that involved torture. Women are very often punitive, though certainly not more so than men, but punitiveness is not bloodthirstiness; it is due partly to fear and partly to an extremely over-simplified conception of justice.

As to the women of savage tribes, when they exhibit bloodthirstiness they are usually carrying out practices which are the law and custom of their clan, frequently with a religious objective and invariably established by gods, kings, chiefs, priests and witch doctors, who, again, are of the masculine, not the feminine, persuasion. And that's that.

But the real significance of Bernard Shaw's lucubration does not lie in his misstatements, however nonsensical. It lies in the moral quality of his make-up, revealed by his article. I am not discussing now his literary works, but the political attitude he has adopted.

Here is an Irishman, poor, and ignored in his own country, who migrates to England and becomes one of the richest, most popular and belauded of English writers. He attacks everybody and everything that does not please him in England and that means every imaginable personality, government, principle, tradition and institution. He flamboyantly defends his right to say exactly what he likes, and is given every permission, and afforded every opportunity, to speak his interminably critical mind; indeed, to bawl it from the housetops. His pocket flourishes; his tastes are satisfied; his intellect is untrammelled.

All these advantages he enjoys in a democratic system which he perpetually smears or tries to tear to shreds. That's bad enough, but he goes further. For what does he uphold? A regime which will perfect all the liberties and privileges which alone make his life worth living, and by which he profits inordinately? Oh dear, no.

He upholds regimes which are the antithesis of the one whose tolerance he exploits. Regimes that suppress free thought, free speech, free conscience; that annihilate defenceless minorities; that put to death without trial; that are based on, inflame and unleash, the instincts rife in man when he was pure beast two or three hundred thousand years ago. He supports Mussolini, he praises Hitler, and he admires, day in and day out, Soviet Russia. He worships the ideas of power, force and despotism. They thrill him, genuinely, to his marrow. He declares openly that they should reign in the world of men.

Now what is the matter with him, that he endorses the evil things in our nature: brutality, barbarism, oppression? He is not personally mean, far from it; nor is he envious, vindictive, touchy, or self-seeking. On many subjects he has a prodigious insight into the human heart.

Of course, on the other hand, he is colossally self-complacent and conceited. But self complacency and conceit, however colossal, do not really bother me. They only show that a man has no self-knowledge, and is therefore incomplete in his intelligence. But none of us is complete in his intelligence. Bernard Shaw just chose, or just was fated, to have deficiencies which make him appear especially silly; and though they may be more irritating, they are not ethically worse than a number of other lacks I could name.

The mischief is deeper. The matter with him is a spirit that is perverted, and an egoism which in its essence is like that of the mad. To champion the creatures and methods he does shows such indifference to human suffering, such a scorn of men's rights, such an approval of injustice, as can only proceed from a vitiated soul. His political philosophy is proof that he is incapable of caring for any ideal and any happiness save the kind peculiar to himself; indulgence in his own comfort, enjoyment in the exercise of his own wit. And that sort of exclusive self-centredness is the hallmark of the unbalanced.

Even his adoration of efficiency, which according to him is the motive of his partiality for tyranny, is shot through with the same inhumanity, since it relates merely to the triumphant imposition of one man's will upon the destiny of millions of others. The efficiency of his idols, the dictators, is only true in so far as the realisation of their own aims of autocracy is concerned; for in what fashion have Fascism, Nazism and Bolshevism procured felicity for the peoples under their thong? The Italians have never been poorer than today; nor the Germans more desperately insecure; nor the Russians more terrorised and enslaved.

Practically, Bernard Shaw's aberrations are of no consequence. He is discrediting himself more and more widely in England; he is hardly known in France; and he has no influence on events and decisions anywhere in the world. He taints very little except himself. But I object to him as an outrageous incongruity. He has no part in any country whose men and women are sacrificing their lives, their interests, their well-being so as to ensure the survival of a civilized order. They labour and they die while he spouts words.

His place is not among them. But I'm damned if I know what to do with him. The democracy under whose protective skirt he sits, doing his pertinacious best to blow her sky-high, is more consistent than he, and won't take a leaf out of his book and shut him up in a concentration camp. He won't repair to those delectable totalitarian lands, Germany, Italy, Russia. It has been suggested to him by [the writer] Geoffrey Garratt that he should rise to one final gesture and lead a pilgrimage of his compatriots back to Ireland. He could then live without danger in the only neutral country which is not threatened; he could sneer at England and France with a German ambassador who'd pass on the new jibes to Lord Haw-Haw; he'd be allowed to take all the money he made in and by England out of England, a move for which Benito, Adolf and Joe would liquidate him instantly if he were their fortunate subject.

But George Bernard flatly refused. Here he is, and here he'll stick until the lord God, who, they say, isn't put off by anything, will develop at long last a yearning for him, and, summoning him home, will decently solve the problem for us all.

*   *   *   *   *

In reply –

Think Odette, Think

by Bernard Shaw

I cannot think that any kindly soul will read all this stuff without being touched by Odette's innocence. She believes that the rampant plutocracies of the West are democracies because they call themselves so. Because I have pointed out that Napoleon III could rebuild Paris and the Duce rebuild Rome while the British House of Commons cannot build a bridge across the [River] Severn, she infers that I delight in concentration camps (which, I may remind her, are a British invention), and proscriptions, and torture, and all the other atrocities which ensue from autocracies because the autocrat cannot be everywhere, and must delegate his powers to blackguards whom he must countenance because their authority is derived from his own.

Because I take pains to show exactly what is wrong with dictatorships and what is wrong with our pseudo-democracies, instead of calling Hitler and Stalin bloodthirsty ruffians (which is merely the pot calling the kettle black), she concludes that I am an anti-Semite and a Heil Hitler enthusiast.

Because I explained in a bellicose magazine under feminine control precisely how women claim to have a strong interest in the fighting qualities of men, she will have it that I regard women as murderous savages and men as angels of mercy. This logic is too salutatory for the existing situation, though it is common enough, worse luck.

On one point Odette is, alas, quite right. The people labour and die while I spout words. But is that my fault? Think, Odette, think!

April 1940

It's Lovely to be Old

by George Lansbury

Old age is lovely for me in spite of the horrors of war, or of personal and family worries. It is pleasant, alone in my thoughts, to live over again the days of adolescence when, with my future wife, and in company with friends, I went cavorting around the deserted streets of the City of London.

Through the joy and troubles of married life, and of a huge family, life was a perpetual honeymoon which broke up disagreements and sent my wife with a smile on her face to carry on the work of housekeeping. It is good to remember we were comrades together in all the great movements of our day. We were never rich in material things, but always very rich in friends who belonged to all classes.

It is good to know that my worrying her by going to prison twice for public causes, and some of my children doing the same, made no difference to her attitude to life. There are a thousand memories such as these which it is grand to live over and remember. My large family of children, children-in-law, grandchildren, great-grandchildren and godchildren are a very big pull on my desire to live.

What old person is there who, blessed with very young relatives, does not find relaxation and joy in their company? I do, even though they completely wear me out, clambering over my bed, demanding a drink of my early tea, or rolling all over my big armchair and me. Urging me to do the impossible; to draw an aeroplane, a ship or an engine. No old person who has lost interest in babies and children can really understand what I mean by joy in old age. We will never die if we are able to impress a cheerful personality on young children.

So to all old people I would say, if you want a happy, a good, old age, grow old without knowing you are doing so. And do this by giving some time to tiny children and talking on terms of equality with them as often as possible. It is good for me to hear the shout for Granddad, even to be worried and troubled about the future of the children I know, because my belief is that evil though our times are, often as evil seems to prosper, the children who survive the present struggle will find their way to a nobler life; a life of co-operative love and service one towards the other. Old age is lovely because of the memory of long years spent in trying to help Poor Law children and the memory of the love and sympathy shown me by these children in after life.

It is good in some ways, though not in all, to look back on the jolly time I had for two years as His Majesty's First Commissioner of Works. Throwing open the Serpentine for mixed bathing, creating a Lido in the centre of London, opening up parks and open spaces, bathing pools and sports grounds, is a great memory for me. As also is the fact that almost without an effort I managed to lift £30,000 from good-hearted people who cared for children.

I look back also on our hard emigrant trip to Queensland and the rough time we passed in town and bush over fifty years ago. I like also to remember the days when I was a cricket fan watching the first Australian team defeat the Marylebone Club at Lords. I can't remember the date, only the match, and lots of others which had a better ending for England.

Then in old age I find it good to pass and re-pass in memory the many noted men and women I have known at home and abroad, and to have learned that in public life a person's reputation often depends upon whether the public agrees with him or not. Time is a great healer as the history of our House of Commons proves.

I have been going to the House of Commons as boy and man, and later as a member, ever since 1874. I have listened to all the famous men and women of my time. I have met and talked with members of the royal family, politicians, cardinals, archbishops, philosophers and every kind of reformer, while abroad I have met kings and dictators, and two presidents of the USA.

I passed two long visits in Russia where I saw a nation being starved of the means of life by a terrible blockade. When I met Lenin, Stalin, Trotsky and others I found myself wondering whence came their power over the Russian masses. I like to remember my discussion of religion with Lenin which he abruptly ended by telling me to go home and convert the English Christians.

I can truthfully say that until the last eighteen months age never troubled me. I was too busy; life was full up with public and personal affairs. Now, coming through the hard winter I have discovered many weak points in my bodily armour. But so far my mind remains young. I find old age good, most of all when nights are long and sleep won't come and memory brings back to me the weekends spent in propaganda work on behalf of the Labour movement.

I have been given hospitality in the homes of miners, cotton operatives, mechanics and labourers, and from their enthusiasm and devotion to great causes I received inspiration and courage to come back to London, knowing I was not alone. It is good, too, to remember my short period as leader of His Majesty's Opposition in the House of Commons, fewer than fifty of us. At first everyone thought us a joke; but our devotion to work, our refusal to believe we were a minority, our determination to preserve democratic life in and out of the House of Commons gives me much satisfaction in these disappointing days.

So my reason for saying, yes, old age is good, is the blessedness of memory, memory of the grievous faith and failures of my life, but chief of all memories of great love and service in company with ordinary people at home and abroad. I look back and find consolation in the thought that, out of the apparent hopelessness of the present time with its threatened slaughter and destruction, a new effort will arise and once again the voice of reason and common sense will be heard and mankind saved by the goodwill of men and women whose only desire is to live at peace and work for their daily bread.

Often I am overborne with trials and many difficulties, but always there comes a moment when I am able to say: "Hitherto has the Lord blessed me, not with money, place or power but with the joy of living as his child, striving to become one of those who serve."

May 1940

A Natural Solution

by Clarisse Meitner

They had met on the train. Trains are the easiest possible places to get to know people. She was going to Dalmatia for a holiday; he was on a business trip to Yugoslavia. They happened to be sharing a compartment from Graz to Zagreb and the hours passed in pleasant conversation. They had the compartment to themselves, so they were able to talk without embarrassment, and being total strangers there was plenty for them to talk about.

They had plenty of time on their hands too, and no other distractions. Anything that relieves the tedium of a journey is welcome and almost any topic of conversation agreeable.

In this particular case there was also an instinctive mutual liking and, on the part of the woman, the kind of excited curiosity that usually accompanies the beginning of a holiday, when one is secretly convinced that something nice is going to happen, that this time fate is going to be kind. Despite all one's previous experiences, one looks forward with confidence to fine weather, pleasant company, good food and cheap prices.

And as well as all this, they had to cross a frontier. So it was not surprising that by the time they reached Maribor they were on the best of terms. For nothing draws strangers together more quickly than having to go through the customs. One stands united against the common foe: the customs official. Whether one has anything to declare or not, and even if one's travelling companion has hitherto seemed insufferable, he instantly becomes an accomplice, a brother; while the customs official, though he may utter his "Have you anything to declare" in the suavest, most helpful accents, is branded finally and irrevocably as the enemy.

But in this case the lady's travelling companion could by no stretch of the imagination have been described as insufferable. He was indeed handsome, courteous, and extremely amusing; a widely travelled man, with a fund of entertaining anecdotes. When he reached his destination and was about to get off the train, they found that the time had simply flown, and they were genuinely sorry to say goodbye.

They were delighted to have made one another's acquaintance; they exchanged names and addresses, promised to exchange picture postcards also, and agreed that should he ever happen to pass through Vienna, which was where she had her home, he would call on her without fail.

And he kept his promise. Some months later (the lady's holiday, incidentally, had been entirely successful and in almost every respect had come up to expectation) a "fortunate coincidence" caused him to visit Vienna "on business." He telephoned her and was invited to tea. He arrived with a bunch of flowers, and a whole lot of new anecdotes and experiences to tell her, so again there was plenty to talk about. She was able to prove that not only was she a delightful travelling companion but an excellent and charming hostess as well.

The tea was beyond praise, her home was comfortable and tastefully furnished, she herself was gay, amusing, and obviously pleased to see him. This time there was no need of a customs official to make it plain that they might become excellent friends.

The following evening they went to the opera, and it was a highly successful evening. The performance could not have been bettered and they were charmed to find that, having already discovered so many interests and tastes in common, they should also share an appreciation of music. On the third day he had to leave.

This time they made no agreement, but, instead of exchanging postcards as they had been doing, they now wrote letters regularly. In the spring he came to Vienna again. He brought a vast bunch of flowers on this occasion and he was invited, not to tea, but to lunch. For some reason he seemed to be a little embarrassed, but his hostess used her very considerable charm to put him at his ease.

Over coffee, he said: "I want to make a suggestion, which you may think rather odd. Would you . . . do you think we could get married? I have to leave Vienna on Monday and it would be nice if you could come with me. I'm going to Italy this time and I should so much love you to see it with me. You, of all people in the world, would appreciate its beauty. Well, will you?" He took her hand and smiled into her eyes.

"But . . . really . . . I mean, how can we? What would people say? I'd like to . . . but it's simply ridiculous . . I'm sorry, I mean . . . I don't really think I could. . . ."

You may be wondering why the lady was so taken aback. After all, it was to be expected. Or was she perhaps just being feminine and coquettish? No . . . a slow girlish blush was spreading over her face. She was embarrassed and a little ashamed, because it must now be revealed that the lady was sixty and the man sixty-five. And yet his proposal was the most natural and simple solution.

July 1940

The Bravest Woman I Know

by Rosita Forbes

I am not sure that I have made up my mind between two very different women. The first is Alexandra Niel, a French provincial housewife who suddenly became a Buddhist, and devoted the rest of her life to the study of religion and magic in Asia.

For fourteen years she lived as a Tibetan nun. In the disguise of a poor peasant, she made the forbidden journey to Lhasa just to show the British Government (which had closed the frontiers) how easily they could be outwitted.

This amazing woman speaks a number of Tibetan dialects, has passed snowbound winters in a mountain cell practising the mastery of mind over flesh, and knows more about occultism as it is familiarly practised on the roof of the world than any other living European.

She has held the chair of Oriental Philosophy at the greatest of French Universities, the Sorbonne, and when she was over sixty she wrote to me from war-shattered, and, of course, triply forbidden Mongolia (where Russia, Japan, and China were involved in mysterious and atrocious struggles). "Life here pleases me. It moves at the pace of my donkey, not of those planes which you so much enjoy. I prefer this, for I am not afraid of wasting time. I am only afraid of not savouring it sufficiently."

A very remarkable woman is Alexandra Niel, who for half a lifetime has faced death by thirst, hunger, exposure or, if her nationality were discovered, by terrible and protracted torture.

Yet, perhaps because action has always appealed to me even more than philosophical reflection, my favourite heroine is the impetuous young Turkish girl, Khalida Khanoum Edib, who played Joan of Arc to Turkey's first great President, Mustapha Kemal.

The child of a good family in Constantinople, she had to evade slaves and guardian eunuchs, when late at night she slipped out of a shuttered window (its bars mysteriously loosened) to conduct feminist and socialist meetings for the 'Young Turk' party. Outlawed by the Sultan, she narrowly escaped the usual fate of rebellious women; being sewn into a sack and drowned in the Bosphorus. The veil and the shapeless cloak then worn by Turkish ladies hid her when she went about her perilous business by day. Her friends, members of various secret societies, working for the liberation of Turkey, hid her by night.

When the Allies occupied Constantinople at the end of the last war, Khalida's arrest as a spy and a subversive agent was ordered. But this surprising girl, brought up to the softness of a harem, escaped our military police as easily as the Sultan's janizaries. On a moonless night, she tried to swim the Bosphorus to join the free Turks still fighting the

Allies under Kemal in Asia Minor. She was picked up half drowned by a fishing-boat and landed on the Anatolian shore.

It was she who inspired Kemal to his daring attack against a huge Greek army with a peasant force outnumbered ten to one. She tore off her veil and tied it to a bayonet as she led a battalion to the rout of the Greeks, driven disorganised to the coast. When the slaughter was over, she returned to Kemal with the blood-stained gauze and demanded as its price the freedom of Turkish women.

The Ghazi made Khalida first Minister of Education in the new peasant republic. But she was as strong-willed and as direct in speech as the man who first worshipped and then betrayed her. Unmoved she saw Smyrna burning with its Greek and Armenian populations, but she could not endure the execution of stalwart friends who had raised the Ghazi to power and subsequently disputed his tyranny.

When the mighty President erected a particularly long line of scaffolds under his palace windows and, in the middle of a bridge hand-signed the death warrants of men who had risked their lives for him, Khalida decided to save what was left to her.

With her life and nothing else she escaped to the coast, was smuggled on board a sailing-boat and eventually reached America. There I met her, still impetuous, dark, restless, the girl who had unveiled half a continent, the woman who had inspired Kemal and been sacrificed to his relentless, but successful, will.

October 1940

Home is the Sailor

by Leslie Halward

It was a chilly evening for June and the tramp's stomach cried out for a can of steaming tea. He possessed a can, an old cocoa tin with a detachable wire handle, but not the necessary ingredients; so at the next cottage he came to he halted, looked round furtively (not because he was afraid of anything in particular but because looking round furtively had become a habit with him), unlatched the gate and slithered rather than walked up the path.

He was a comparatively respectable looking tramp, no more untidy in his appearance than a good many labourers and with only two days' growth of stubble on his chin; so he was surprised when the pleasant-looking fifty-year-old woman who opened the door in answer to his knock took one look at him, gave a cry, and fell across her own threshold in a dead faint.

The tramp, open-mouthed, gazed at her for some seconds, wondering what he had better do. His first impulse was to bolt, because, even in so quiet a place, somebody might appear suddenly, see the pair of them like that, the woman on the floor and he standing over her, assume that he had assaulted her and, without waiting for an explanation, do him bodily harm. But even while he was thinking this, the woman opened her eyes and tried to get to her feet.

She was deathly white and trembled violently as the tramp put a hand under her arm to help her up. She drew three or four long breaths, all the time not taking her wide eyes from the tramp's face, and then whispered the single word: "George."

Now the tramp's name was not George but Fred; Fred Monk, but he did not tell the woman so. He still felt he ought to run for it, but he kept his feet firmly planted and his mouth shut; for his quick mind had taken in the situation and it had occurred to him that he might profit by it. This woman, who seemed to be alone in the house, had mistaken him for somebody else. If that somebody else was a welcome visitor he would be received kindly. If not, well then would be the time to point out the mistake in identity. So he waited, looking steadily at the woman until she spoke again.

"George. After all these years. I can't believe it." Whoever George was, he had a warm place in the woman's heart, for her voice was husky with emotion and her smile was a smile of pure joy. "Is it really you?" Fred nodded. "Yes, it's me," he said.

"It's wonderful, wonderful," the woman breathed. "George." She said once more, and she threw her arms about him and held him tight, smothering his face with kisses and laughing and crying all at the same time, causing Fred such embarrassment that all but his last bit of courage deserted him. But he put behind him the urge to take to his heels. The smell of cooking tantalised his nostrils and made him swallow his gastric juices. "I'll get a meal out of the old girl," he told himself, "and then I'll take my hook."

"But come in, do," the woman said, releasing him. "A man shouldn't be kept on the doorstep of his own home, even if it is twenty years since he entered it!" She laughed like a girl and, taking his hand, led him into the kitchen. "Take off your things and sit down by the fire there. Your chair's just where it was the day you went from here. You'll find everything where you left it, for somehow I could never believe you were dead. Sit you down, now. The supper's all but ready and as soon as Jim comes in I'll serve it up. My, won't he have a shock. You won't know him, of course, for he was little more than a baby when you went away. Oh, but this is a wonderful day, for after twenty years the good Lord's sent you back to me."

To all this Fred was only half listening, for his eyes were glued on a photograph that hung on the wall over the dresser. It was a photograph of himself as a young man, dressed up in a sailor's uniform. It wasn't really himself, of course, it was George, this woman's husband, who was dead and whom his wife now thought had been delivered back to her. "So I'm a sailor," Fred thought. "That's a bit rich."

He took off his things and sat down in the old-fashioned armchair by the fireside. The woman fussed about him and chattered without ceasing, giving him a clue here and there as to the fate of George and the sort of man he used to be. He listened, saying nothing, and picked out bits of information. He was determined now to keep up the pretence until after he'd had a helping of that stew.

There was a clatter of hobnailed boots on the path and a moment later a young man with the grace and proportions of an ox stamped into the room. "Jim!" his mother cried, going to him and gripping his arm with her plump red hands. "I've got a surprise for you! Oh, such a surprise as never was." She turned her beaming gaze on Fred, who wriggled uncomfortably and examined the cracked toe of his boot. "That," she said, "is your father, your poor dear father who we thought was drowned in the sea more than twenty years ago."

She watched her son's face to see the effect of this bombshell. There wasn't any effect to speak of. Jim's mouth opened perhaps a quarter of an inch wider than it was at ordinary times. Certainly he looked as if he didn't believe what he had been told, but then he always looked like that. He strode across the room, stood in front of Fred, held out a hand as big as a horse's hoof, and said: "How are yer?"

Fred half-rose, took the hand, winced as his own was almost crushed, and said: "I'm all right son. How's yerself?" Without answering, Jim rattled off into the scullery and made a great row washing himself. Fred had made up his mind that when he had eaten the meal that the three of them shared he would make an excuse to go out of the room and take his leave of the simple couple while the going was good.

But the stew and potatoes and the bread pudding, rich with currants and sultanas, he had eaten had made him feel so pleasantly drowsy that the thought of any sort of activity was extremely distasteful to him. He sat with half-closed eyes, watching the woman clear the things, ignoring the son who sat gaping at him from the other side of the fireplace, and sighed a sigh of deep satisfaction. He took from a pocket an old pipe, the bowl burnt half away, filled it with tobacco salvaged from cigarette ends, and lit up. This was comfort, luxury, such as he had not experienced for years.

"And now," the woman said, when at last the dirty plates had been washed and put back in the cupboard, "tell us all about what happened to you. Tell us where you've been; everything." It was the moment Fred had been dreading until a few minutes ago, when he had had an inspiration.

"Well," he said, very deliberately, "the trouble is I lost me memory. I can't remember nothing. Nothing much, that is. I can recollect one or two things. But not a lot. The blow I had on me head with the lanyard when the ship went down it must've cracked me brain. I only just found out who I was about a month ago, when I was in Singapore, and I come straight home. I keep remembering bits and it'll come back by and by. It's all muddled up just now."

"I can't recollect whether it was California or Armentieres where I swum ashore. Or it might've been Spain. I couldn't say, not now. Later it'll come back and then I'll be able to tell you the lot. But it's no good now. Not a bit. I'm all muzzy-like from that blow I had on the head with the lanyard. It must've cracked me brain, it must." He shut his eyes up tight and kept them like that for about a minute. Then he opened them again, shook his head three or four times, and said: "No, it's no good. All the things in me mind is cluttered up together like as if somebody stirred them with a spoon."

"Tell us how you got from Singapore when you found out who you was," the woman suggested. So he told them how he got from Singapore, how he worked his passage to India in a coffee barge, and then crossed the Alps alone, and by and by made his way, more dead than alive, to the Dutch coast. The narrative lasted an hour, and at the end of it he felt too weary to move, for the labour of invention had tired him out. And before he knew what was happening, the woman had lit a couple of candles and blown out the lamp. It was time, she said, that they went to bed.

George has been home now for nearly a year, and little by little his memory is returning. The villagers call him Captain and most evenings he can be heard in the *Ewe and Lamb*, where he hardly ever pays for a drink, recounting his astonishing adventures in incredible places as the consumption of one pint after another sets his cracked brain working. He is popular and happy, for he lives, comparatively, like a lord. Twice during the spring he experienced an almost overpowering desire to take to the road again. But now the urge has left him. He is settled and very content.

October 1940

Empire Hero

by John Peskett

Soon after the Gordon Memorial was erected in Khartoum, an officer stationed there took his little son to see it. He told the boy about the deeds which had won the Empire. He pointed up at Gordon, sitting on his camel looking out across Africa. The boy listened, looking at the statue in admiration. Then his father stepped back and saluted Gordon.

And he taught the little lad to salute Gordon. "Every time you pass by here, my son, remember Gordon and salute him." The boy learned to salute the memorial and his father's breast filled with pride of Empire as he watched the lad draw himself up and salute smartly. "He'll grow up with a fine appreciation of all the Empire means to us." he thought, and the little ceremony took place every time they passed that way.

Whether he was with his father or not, the little boy never failed to salute Gordon. When his father was with him, he always gave him a short parental lecture on the greatness of the Empire. Gordon became an outstanding figure in the boy's mind and his father dreamed of the great man his own son would become.

Time passed and the soldier's son had to leave for England to go to school. He took leave of his friends and then his father led him to the Gordon Memorial for the last time. He stood at attention, saluted bravely and marched off under the proud eye of his father.

But on the boat, the boy seemed troubled and his father asked why. "You've said goodbye very bravely to all your friends and you've said goodbye to Gordon. And I know you will always remember Gordon." he said. His soldierly breast was full of emotion as he thought of the Empire and how he had instilled in the boy an admiration of one of its builders.

"Yes," said the boy, "but there was one thing I wanted to ask you. "What is it, my boy?" asked his father.

"Well, daddy, who is the gentleman on Gordon's back?"

August 1941

Germany Calling

by Richard Darwall

He had been an announcer at Radio Luxembourg before the war. When it came he had gone home and enlisted at once and found himself allocated to an infantry regiment. In March his unit was sent to France, and in May, when the offensive started, moved up into Belgium with the rest of the British Expeditionary Force. Then, as the retreat began, his unit moved back, towards the coast. But his regiment never reached the sea. One evening, as they fought their way back, bombed from the air, bombarded from the front and flanks, the firing came suddenly from yet another quarter: the rear. A Panzer division had cut them off.

All that night he and his comrades held the enemy off, fought them until a battalion had become a company, a company a platoon, until their last round was fired and they were surrounded and helpless. And so, nine weeks after he had landed in France, he was on his way to Germany as a prisoner of war.

The prison camp was somewhere in Bavaria. One by one he and his comrades filed into the camp commandant's office. "Name. Unit. Home Address. Occupation." The typewriter tapped out their brief dossiers dispassionately. "Radio announcer" The camp commandant glanced up at him for a moment, but made no comment.

Three months passed. Three months of grinding boredom and futility, as the brilliant summer dragged on. Writing letters that brought no answers, expecting parcels that never came. The vile doldrums, the heart-sapping ennui of prison life. How long could this go on? Through how many more dreary days, months, years?

Then, one day in September, the break came. The orderly called out his name in the barrack room, and led him to the prison office. He stood to attention before the camp commandant's desk.

"You were a radio announcer before the war?" "Yes, sir."

"You like prison life?" "Hardly." "Well, here is your chance to get out. We can use you to broadcast our official communiques in English. Nothing more than that. If you accept you will be free, on parole. You will go to Berlin, live the life of a free man. What do you say?" What could he say? What was he to say? On the one side lay freedom, of a sort; on the other captivity, unendurable, seemingly unending. The commandant saw his hesitation: "Think it over. I'll send for you again in three days."

When he came up before the commandant again he accepted. They took him to Berlin by car and lodged him in an hotel off the Unter den Linden. Next day they took him to the broadcasting studios. There it all was, the neat little microphone, the desk with its shaded lamp and glass of water, the comfortable chair. Everyone was very polite to him, almost solicitous. No hint of a threat anywhere, nor of irony.

"We're going to give you a voice test. You won't be on the air," they told him, and put a typed sheet on the desk before him. "Watch the clock," the suave announcer said, "and start reading when the minute hand of the clock is at twelve." He glanced at the sheet. It was a High Command communique announcing raids on Hull, Portsmouth and London, followed by an account of shipping sunk in the Atlantic. Just a bald statement of what the Propaganda Ministry wanted the world to regard as facts. He began to read in the even, unemphatic voice he'd been taught to read news bulletins.

Halfway through the announcer held up his hand. "Give it more emphasis, you sound too flat," he said. He nodded and read on to the end, raising his voice here and there a little. What did it matter after all, he thought afterwards. It wasn't me reading that stuff. It was just a voice going over the ether. No man behind it. Nothing but a voice out of the void. No one believes it, anyway. The test was all right, they told him. They took him to a concert afterwards.

Next evening he went to the studio again. This time it was to be the real thing. They brought him up there in plenty of time before the broadcast. Had they recorded the test, he asked. They had. Could they run it through for him? Certainly.

Then he heard his own voice come over through the loudspeaker, flat at first, as the announcer had said, but later with more emphasis. His heart clutched. It sounded good. It sounded real, true, sincere. That was how they would hear it over in his country. All those damned distorted facts, read clearly, calmly, but with due emphasis in an English voice, his voice. Maybe the sirens would have sounded; the bombs be already dropping as his voice reached them over there.

It was time to get ready, they said. He sat down at the desk and picked up the script. The red warning light flashed on and the minute hand of the clock flickered round the dial. He began to read: "Germany calling. This is Germany calling. Last night the Luftwaffe carried out extensive raids over Southampton, Merseyside and London. Heavy fires .....

Suddenly he stopped, leaned close towards the microphone. "Down with Hitler. The hell with Hitler." he yelled at the top of his voice. A swift shadow moved behind him and he went down to a crashing blow between the eyes.

December 1941

Goodbye Romano's

by James Agate

"Romano's?" said one of our modern sprigs, looking up from his evening paper. "Isn't that the place opposite Heppell's?" And very quietly I began to tell him of the past. Of the absurd and grandiose decor of the old place, compensated by the sensible and discreet alcoves. Of the admirable food, the first-class wine list, the punctual and punctilious waiting, with no damned nonsense about the equality of man. Here were obsequiousness and subservience, cringing and servility; everything that the old Romans knew, and 'the Roman' had no intention of forgetting.

As I write, my eye catches some words of Leo Amery. "Pre-war notions and theories will be out of date after this war. There will be no room for theoretical individuals or socialists, for die-hard Tories or die-hard Trade Unionists. Undoubtedly we shall want a much better organisation of our whole political and social structure."

I know the kind of thing. Today I shall have my food thrown at me by some garlic-reeking Soho tough; tomorrow it will be my job to throw food at the tough. Turn and turn about; we are all equal and nobody tips anybody. No, thank you. When that happens I shall live permanently in the past. And in that past will largely figure Romano's, where will be gathered together Arthur Roberts, George Sims, George Augustus Sala, Phil May, Arthur Shirley, William Wills, Edmund Yates and many more.

If one wanted to coin a phrase to sum up this particular coterie it would be *The Pink 'Un* crowd. Yet to the world of today such a phrase would mean nothing. Our modern sprig doubtless regards *The Pink 'Un* as the pill one took at the chemist's opposite on emerging from Romano's. To the young man of to-day *Pitcher* [Arthur Binstead], *Swears* [Ernest Wells] and *The Dwarf of Blood* [Nathaniel Newnham-Davis] mean nothing. They are gone, defunct, back numbered and na-pooh'd. They are one with Tyre, Sidon and Ally Sloper, the last of whom encompassed in one sentence the entire works of the current satirists. This is the sentence: "A dirty mind," remarked the Dook Snook, "is a perpetual feast."

What a master of the anecdote, the short story, the epigram, the innuendo, the salacity was *Pitcher*. And how well he wears. How full-blooded in these anaemic days. Yet the best story that I know is told not by, but of, *Pitcher*, He left instructions in his will that after his cremation at Golders Green his friends were to repair to a tavern and carouse at his expense. They did so. As they emerged into the East wind and the cock-eyed dusk one of them called the attention of the party to a thick, flat streaming column of smoke proceeding from the crematorium chimney. "Look," he said. "There's old *Pitcher* going up West for the evening."

The world today is full of an odd and curiously evanescent kind of celebrity which, male or female, smirks from the pages of the illustrated weeklies for one week, thereafter to be seen no more. You cannot tell by looking at a man whether he is a Cabinet Minister, a fashionable actor, a highly paid football player, a gigolo, or the younger brother of a gossip writer. You cannot tell from her looks, manners, talk or perfume whether a woman is a duchess, a ballet dancer, an usherette or a stenographer.

In Romano's day things were not so. People were different from one another. It is true that women wore the same leg-of-mutton sleeves, the same 'buns,' and the same monstrously absurd sailor hats. But like

Ophelia with her rue, they wore these same things with a difference. They had the secret of individual elegance. Each had her own fragrance. Today all that has gone; and gone, I am afraid, for ever.

It would be a great mistake to confound Romano's crowd with that which foregathered at the Cafe Royal. Though contemporaneous, a full decade separated them; the decade between the eighties and nineties. Romano's crowd was rich, well-born and uneducated in the Cafe Royal sense. It had forgotten what little spelling it had learned at Eton, but it knew its way about wine lists, could recite the pedigrees of famous racehorses by the hour, and was an equally good judge of quality in the paddock or on the dance floor. It lived the life that the crowd in Regent Street was finding phrases for.

"I cried for madder music and for stronger wine," wrote Ernest Dowson, meaning that he had hardly enough money to call for coffee and a slice in a cabman's shelter. But when, in the Strand, some peer of the realm called for jeroboams instead of magnums and cigars six inches longer than before we may be sure he got them. Was it all a little vulgar? Yes, in the sense that life in Rome in the great days of Caesars and circuses, and life in Paris at the time of Choderlos de Laclos's *Les Liaisons Dangereuses*, and again in the sixties and the heyday of the demi-monde which young Dumas pretended to denounce, and life at the top in all great capitals at all times in the world's history has been a little vulgar.

And now a politician tells us that we are going to alter all this. Well, I just don't believe it. I believe that one of man's first and entirely natural instincts is the gambling one. I believe that the whole of Rochdale is content to go on being Rochdale because a Rochdale girl once rose to be a music hall star with the world at her feet. I believe that millions of English girls are content to lead a life of grinding virtue in the most sordid conditions because of a Coral Pearl who, once every hundred years or so, finds a Bill Blinkwell to take her to Paris and leave her, at the age of fifteen, to sink or swim in the plashing fountain of Parisian gallantry.

I believe that inequality is part and parcel of the destiny of mankind, and that that state of society is doomed in which there are no vulgar rich to hand out half-crowns and half-sovereigns to entirely undeserving hangers-on and kerb-whiners. Romano's stood for the Burgundy of Bohemianism as opposed to the Bordeaux of the Cafe Royal. It was a full-bodied and full-blooded Tom Tiddler's ground; you knew the game and you stuck to the rules.

It had nothing in common with your modem shady little joints, the Blue Monkeys and Scalded Cats, which are gone tomorrow and are hardly here today. It stood open for all the world. It was a place to take ambassadors to, and in which to discover the budding plenipotentiary. It was essentially Edwardian, and will, I trust, when it opens again, continue to be Edwardian.

"Cocoa," said my friend, the late lamented Basil Macdonald Hastings, "cocoa is unwhisperable." Unwhisperable would be the word for a Romano's which should have lost its panache, its flaunting advertisement that within its walls are to be found that which the greater part of humanity has held to be the best of life. In the words of that great wiseacre, La Fontaine, *bon souper, bon gîte et le reste*. Except, of course, that the entertainment provided by Romano's stopped with the supper. But it was a warm, cosy world they sent you out into to look for the rest.

April 1941

Edward Grieg and the Cigar

by Irene Morris

The other evening some of Edward Grieg's beautiful music from *Peer Gynt* was played on the wireless, and listening to it, a story that my grandmother told me many years ago came into my mind. My grandfather was the Danish consul in Gothenburg, Sweden, the town where I was born and brought up. My grandfather's best and closest friend was Edward Grieg who, when he was visiting Sweden and giving concerts in Gothenburg, always stayed in my grandparents' home.

One Sunday evening after one of Grieg's big concerts, he invited my grandparents for supper at the Grand Hotel. They arrived at the hotel, entered the dining-room and sat down at their table without anyone recognising Grieg. After their meal Grieg took up a cigar and lit it. In those days nobody smoked in a dining-room in a first-class hotel in Sweden, but Grieg was Norwegian and knew nothing about this. A waiter immediately came up to him and told him in rather an abrupt manner that he was not allowed to smoke his cigar.

Grieg first looked surprised, then shrugged his shoulders and, completely ignoring the waiter's remark, calmly kept on smoking. The waiter at once went out and fetched the head waiter, who arrived looking very self-confident. By now everybody in the dining-room was staring at Grieg, who in a very loud and singing Norwegian voice kept talking to my grandparents. Some of the guests plainly showed their disgust over this man, who indeed was behaving disgracefully by smoking a cigar in the dining-room of a first-class hotel.

When the head waiter came up to Grieg's table, there was an intense quietness at all the other tables and everybody could hear him say: "I beg your pardon, sir, but smoking is not allowed in the dining-room, and I must ask you to put out your cigar."

Grieg, who sometimes had a very fiery temper, told him he would not stop smoking his cigar no matter what was allowed or not allowed. The head waiter, red in the face with anger, told Grieg that he would have to leave the dining-room if he insisted on smoking, and a few of the guests joined in the conversation, warmly agreeing with the head-waiter. At this my grandfather, white with fury, rose from his seat and announced in a loud voice: "Gentlemen, do you realise that you are talking to Edward Grieg."

There was a few seconds of startled quietness then everybody began talking at the same time. The head waiter bowed to the ground, apologising, stuttering and bowing again. Of course Herr Grieg was allowed to smoke. How absurd to think that anyone could object to that. Really, Herr Grieg. The hotel; the guests; yes, the whole town was overwhelmed by the honour of having Herr Grieg as their guest.

There was a minute or two of chaos, and the air was buzzing with humble apologies. The head waiter offered Grieg a better table, and asked if he might have the honour of presenting a bottle of fine old wine; Chateau la Tour 1870, the pride of the Grand Hotel. Anything, anything for Herr Grieg.

But Herr Grieg was by now rather tired of the whole affair, dismissed the bowing head waiter, asked for his bill and left the dining-room with my shocked and rather upset grandparents. From that day on smoking was allowed in all dining-rooms in every first-class hotel in Sweden.

April 1941

The Best Policy

by Ferenc Molnar

Monsieur Bayout, President of the National Farmers Bank, sent for his secretary Philibert one morning. "Tell me, Philibert," he said, "who is this man Floriot down at our Perpignan branch?"

"Floriot? That's the cashier. He's acting as manager temporarily. You remember, sir, the old manager, Boucher, died, and we haven't found anyone to put in his place yet. Floriot's looking after things meanwhile. There isn't very much business in Perpignan."

Monsieur Bayout took a letter from his desk. "Well, apparently he's robbing us. I've had this letter from Perpignan. It's anonymous, I admit, but . . ." He handed Philibert a not very clean sheet of notepaper on which, in a somewhat unformed hand, the following lines were written:

'To the President of the National Farmers Bank. Dear Sir, We farmers are putting our hard earned savings in your bank at Perpignan, and one fine day we shall wake up and find it has gone bankrupt and all our savings are lost. It is bound to happen the way things are going on here. You probably don't know that the cashier, Monsieur Floriot, has been embezzling money for months past. He must have put away a tidy packet by now, but of course by the time you high and mighty gentlemen in Paris realise what is going on, all the money will be gone.'

"Send an inspector down to Perpignan tomorrow, Philibert," the President said. "But tell him to be tactful, we don't want to upset the man. There's probably no foundation for the story."

Monsieur Floriot, temporary manager of the Perpignan branch, stared at the inspector from Paris with horrified amazement. "Inspect my books?" he echoed. "What, now? In the middle of the month? Without any notification? It's a bit unusual, isn't it?"

The inspector felt sorry for the agitated little man. "There's nothing to worry about, Monsieur Floriot. We do this at all our branches from time to time. The President gets these sudden fits. It's only a formality. I'll be through in half an hour."

"Yes! but people will talk, especially in a small place like this," Floriot wailed. "Everyone will be saying that I've been up to something shady. The disgrace, think of the disgrace."

"Nobody's going to know anything about it," the inspector said, a trifle impatiently. "That is, of course, unless you yourself talk. Well, can I see the books now?"

Two days later Philibert entered the President's room. "I'm able to report on the inspector's visit to Perpignan, sir. Everything is in order. Not a single sou missing."

"Good. One really ought not to pay any attention to these disgusting anonymous letter-writers. Thanks, Philibert."

Less than a month later, the President again summoned his secretary. "It's quite ridiculous," he said testily. "But I've had another anonymous letter about Perpignan. The writer declares that the books weren't properly examined. Apparently Floriot made such a song and dance about the whole thing that an accomplice had time to replace the stolen money. We really ought to have gone into the matter more thoroughly."

"Do we have to make another investigation?" Philibert asked ruefully.

The President drummed his fingers on the desk. "I don't like doing it. All the same, it's a duty we owe to our clients. If there is something in it, and people find out afterwards that we were warned, there'll be a nasty scandal. I'm afraid the only thing to do is send the inspector down again. And this time let him do the job thoroughly. I want to clear this up once and for all."

The same day three of the bank's most reliable inspectors set out for

Perpignan. This time Monsieur Floriot was really taken by surprise. One of the officials kept guard over him, while the other two carried out a thorough examination of his accounts, lasting over four hours. They found nothing missing, and the books in perfect order. "I only wish things were as satisfactory in all our branches," the chief inspector said, as he bade farewell to the completely shattered Floriot.

A week later: "Monsieur Floriot of Perpignan is waiting to see you, sir," Philibert announced.

Departing from his usual habit, Monsieur Bayout rose and advanced towards his visitor with an outstretched hand. Floriot, however, gave a stiff little bow. "I've come to hand in my resignation, sir," he said. "Your resignation? You can't mean that, my dear Floriot. Why?"

"You found it necessary to have my books examined twice running, sir. Naturally it caused a lot of talk. Even though I was proved to be an honest man, it made a bad impression. People are saying there must have been some good reason why the head office sent down twice to have my affairs investigated. My reputation's gone. I'm not a young man and I have a wife to think of."

Monsieur Bayout was deeply moved. "I'll make it my personal responsibility to see that your name is cleared. Wait a minute, though. . . . The manager's job is still vacant, would you like to have it? No one could doubt your honesty then, could they? Yes, and you'll get a pretty substantial increase in salary, too"

"You really mean . . ." Floriot stammered. "Of course, of course, my dear fellow. The bank will be fortunate in keeping the services of so conscientious a worker."

Back at his home in Perpignan, Pierre Floriot slid his feet into the comfortable felt slippers his wife handed him. "At last." he grunted, in a good humoured voice. "What's the use of being an honest man if nobody hears it? I might have gone on being a cashier for years and years, and the people at head office would never have known how honest I was."

"They know now!" Madame Floriot beamed, regarding her husband with admiration. "Those letters were a wonderful idea of yours."

May 1941

Christmas in Vienna

by Gerald Tyrwhitt-Wilson

I cannot remember having experienced any Christmas that was actually bad except, of course, as regards the weather. But there is one Christmas that remains deeply fixed in my memory; a strange and, in view of subsequent events, a portentous one.

Many years ago I was staying in Vienna with my friend Professor Winzinger, art connoisseur and, at that time, President of the Kunstverein. It was Christmas Day and we were assembled round the Christmas tree. All of a sudden a young man bounced into the room with a large portfolio under his arm.

"Gott en Himmel" exclaimed the Professor. "Why has he come at this time?" He explained to me that the young man was an artist, and that he had promised to look at some of his drawings and give judgment on them. The Frau Professor, a kindly woman, begged her husband not to send the man away, and the Professor, rather reluctantly, examined the contents of the portfolio.

"No, young fellow," he said finally, shaking his head, "I'm afraid you'll never be any good as an artist. I advise you to take up some other profession."

Whereupon the young man began to behave in a most peculiar fashion. He gnashed his teeth, his eyes flashed, and he started to deliver an extraordinary, incoherent speech to the effect that he was destined to play a great part in the history of the world, if not in Art, then in some other way. "I shall make the world tremble" he shouted, and then he threw himself on the floor and began tearing the carpet with his teeth.

"Good gracious" I said to the Professor, as the young man was borne from the room. "Who was that?"

"I understand his name is Adolf Schickelgruber," replied the Professor. "I must apologise for the incident."

January 1942

The Greatest Blimp of Them All

by Victor Pritchett

"It is magnificent, but it is not war," exclaimed the French general, with his nation's genius for creating new cliches, when he witnessed the Charge of the Light Brigade at Balaclava. And English opinion, always so peculiarly elevated by our defeats and debacles, echoed the words. The Poet Laureate wrote a famous poem. It was a far more popular poem than its successor, *The Charge of the Heavy Brigade*, which happened to be a far more successful charge.

In one sense the battle of Balaclava was not a battle against the Russians, but an episode in a war between two brothers-in-law who were also two English peers. In disagreement all their life, Lord Lucan and Lord Cardigan found themselves with high cavalry commands at the British supply base of Balaclava, both of them in their fifties and both of them peace time soldiers who had never seen a shot fired in battle. No two more disastrous appointments have been made in the British Army.

Lord Lucan had brains, but they were of the disputatious kind which were quite incapable of accepting an order without a query about it. Lord Cardigan was a charming but preposterous egotist, a spoiled child with a violent temper, undeniably courageous but never able to see beyond the end of a very fine and distinguished nose. It was enough for Lucan to hear that Cardigan had been given command of the Light Cavalry Brigade, for Lucan to pull all the strings possible in order to get the whole cavalry division and be top dog over his brother-in-law.

Contemporaries compared them to two rival lawyers; Lord Lucan intense, "like a panther about to spring with a fierce tearing energy on his opponent," in the words of Alexander Kinglake, the unsparing but just historian of the campaign and Lord Cardigan a blue-eyed, handsome sahib, long in the fork and stiff in the saddle, whose noble, hawk-like mien disguised the small pettifogging mind of a contented solicitor.

Before he became the hero of the Light Brigade, Cardigan was famous as the most quarrelsome and litigious officer in the British Army. In his passion, his barrenness of mind, and his courage, he became the prototype of all Blimps, fantastic in his egotism, superb in inexperience, as persistent but as dull as a mole.

He owed his rapid rise in rank to the purchase system and to royal influence. In two years he held one-hundred and five courts-martial and made more than seven hundred arrests: the strength of his regiment was three-hundred and fifty men. His quarrels were incalculable. He would force a row about the colour of a bottle; or blow up with rage about the size of a teacup. At last he was obliged to resign; but the Duke of Wellington got him back again. The fact is that Cardigan was essentially a very orderly man; and in a minor position, say as quartermaster, he would have been admirable. But he thought his regiment belonged to him personally. He fitted it out, bought its horses out of his own money, and, when he went to the Crimea, he went out on his own yacht.

One of his first engagements on arriving was not, of course, against the Russians; it was against his commanding officer, his hated brother-in-law. Lucan, like every officer, did not see why Cardigan should regard the war as a private expedition of his own and retire every night to his yacht and eat the meals prepared for him by his French cook. But no criticism ever affected Cardigan. As long as he could show that he was, so to speak, legally within his rights, he simply could not understand what all the fuss was about. He was as self-centred as a child and with all a child's violence, sedulousness and innocence.

But for his heroism in the famous Charge, the story of Lord Cardigan at Balaclava would be one of the greatest military farces in history. When the Heavies were closely engaged with the Russian cavalry, who far outnumbered them, Cardigan with his Light Brigade stood by without raising a hand to help. He cursed his luck, but he was happy in the knowledge that the orders said he was to defend his position if the Russians approached it, and not, as was happening, if they approached the Heavies and exposed a flank. Typically, he was concerned with the enemy only when they attacked him.

The unexpected and unprovided for had never happened in peacetime manoeuvres; therefore it had no right to happen in war. When he was rebuked afterwards, he was not at all dismayed. He produced his brother-in-law's orders and once more had the satisfaction of showing how right he was.

And so he was always right, until, just before the famous Charge, he lost his temper. Lord Raglan, the Commander-in-Chief, had sent orders by one Nolan for cavalry to attack the heights where the Russians were emplaced and to recover the British guns lost earlier in the battle. This order came to Lucan. But Lucan always disputed every order he got. Nolan taunted Lucan with hesitation. He waved his arm and cried, "There is your enemy."

At this Lucan's temper went. The words of the written orders went out of his mind, he took the wave of Nolan's arm to indicate the position to be attacked. Unhappily that casual gesture seemed to indicate not the Russian heights and the lost British guns, but the valley which ran down between the Russian batteries. Lucan hastily chose soldiers for the sacrifice. His choice fell upon his brother-in-law's command.

For a moment Cardigan behaved perfectly. His expression was exalted. He looked like a regal Quixote in his tight pelisse covered with gold lace. His charger was a thoroughbred chestnut with two white legs, unmistakable in the melee. He knew quite well the order he had received was monstrous, but his voice was dignified before his certain martyrdom. Quietly he said, "The brigade will advance." But at this sombre and heroic moment, a horrible farce intervened in Cardigan's career.

As the men trotted off to their death, Nolan, who saw the mistake, rode down across their line, shouting in the din and waving across their line to the correct position. All thoughts of death and danger left Cardigan. He saw only one thing: there had been a breach of military etiquette. Someone was presuming to take the leadership from him in his private war. He cursed Nolan, and in that moment Nolan was fatally hit and carried by his frightened horse, shrieking through Cardigan's ranks. It was a death shriek of despair, a terrible cry, which Cardigan in his rage took to be a further insulting interference.

Although ordered to advance slowly, Cardigan began to gallop his horse. The Charge was on. It was more like a horse race, with Cardigan in his rage, far ahead of his men, breaking through the Russian gunners to their rear and going so fast that he found himself alone among the retreating Cossacks. They attacked him but they were too astonished by the strange sight of this mad gorgeous figure to fight seriously. Both they and his lordship thought discretion the better part. And now comes the singular part of the story. Lord Cardigan rode back.

He had lost touch with his men or, in his rage, had he really forgotten them? No sign of his regiment, he said, could he see. So the commanding officer, who might be supposed to be responsible for rallying his men and ordering their movements, just simply called it a day and rode back home down the valley among the corpses. Was he conscious of his heroism, was he brooding upon the martyrdom of his regiment, was he thinking in awe of his miraculous survival, was he even considering the military position? He was doing none of these things.

The most explosive officer the British Army has ever known arrived before his commander calling for the blood of the officer who had had the impertinence to run across his line when it was moving into action. Five hundred dead he could forget, he could forget his own danger and be unaware of his own courage; but a point of order; that was bigger than the war itself.

Replying to his critics, he pointed out triumphantly that he had not abandoned his men; he had ridden back slowly, but with decorum. "By Gad, sir" (they must have said), "Lord Cardigan is right."

He won all his points of order in the legal battle that followed, and, like all the Blimps who have succeeded him, till his dying day he never noticed how great was his gift for irrelevance.

September 1942

The Enemies of France

by Stanley Howard

The old man scraped the mud from off his sabots and looked lovingly at the low, white-washed buildings of his farm, which lay a few miles south of Paris. The rain fell softly and steadily, with a mist climbing up from the river as dusk drew in. He entered the house, and clattered along the tiled passage to the kitchen. His wife looked up from laying the table. "What has happened?"

"Those English did their job well. There will be no work done there for weeks to come," he told her. "It is good news," she replied, "now put on your slippers, and eat this soup."

As they sat at their meal, the old man recounted to his wife the vast damage done by the Royal Air Force in their raid over Paris the night before. Suddenly there was a knocking at the back door. He made as if to rise. "No, you are tired. I will go." His wife left the room, to return a moment later, her eyes shining with excitement. "There is an English officer outside who wants to know if you will hide him and his men."

"How do you know he is English?" Suspicion was in the old man's voice. "But, Jean, he said so, and he is dressed in English uniform," she told him.

"I will go and see him." He picked up a large lantern that stood on the dresser; lit it, and made silently for the back door. He stopped for a while, listening then flinging it open and raising the lantern; he peered into the darkness, and asked softly, "You wish?"

A tall figure clad in battledress stepped into the wavering circle of light. In excellent French the officer asked for shelter for himself and his men. "You are how many?"

"Seven in all. We were dropped by parachute during last night's raid over Paris. We have carried out our programme and now await an aeroplane to take us back, but we are ahead of schedule, and it will not be here until tomorrow night. Can you hide us for twenty-four hours?"

The old man looked the speaker over from head to heel. "Follow me," he said, after a moment's pause and led the way to the dairy. In the floor to one side of the white-washed building was a trapdoor. "You will be quite safe down there. We will bring you food and water, but," said the old man, "I must ask you all to give me up your weapons.

"Why," asked the officer. "Because if you are discovered, which is not likely, but if you are and have no weapons on you, I shall not get into so much trouble. I can then say, truly, that I disarmed you. Have no fear, I will return them all to you before you go.

"All right." Grudgingly the officer complied, and as he and his men filed down the opening they, one by one, laid down their pistols, ammunition and tommy-guns. The old man closed the trapdoor and stood upon it. He picked up one of the guns, his finger caressing the trigger. "You are new since my day," his voice fell softly, "I wonder if you are so very different? I wonder."

The following morning, in a room at the Gestapo headquarters in Paris, an excited company of officials were discussing the RAF raid. "Someone must have guided the planes with lights. We must find out who and how. They . . " The speaker broke off suddenly, and all sprang to their feet as a highly placed officer of the Gestapo entered.

"So you want to find the traitors who guided our enemies?" he said. "Good. I have arranged a trap. It is this: small contingents of men, each led by an officer and posing as British soldiers, are visiting all outlying farms in the district south of Paris and asking to be hidden until they can be fetched by aeroplane."

"I have here a list of farms and their occupants. Twenty were visited last night. If shelter is refused, good; if accepted, one of the men is to escape and go at once to our local headquarters, fetch the police and arrest the farmer red-handed. Then, so much the worse for him. I await the results now."

The door opened and a soldier stood at the salute. "Herr Commandant, a French peasant is outside. He says he must see you at once." "Bring him up." As the soldier left the room the officer turned to the assembled company with a complacent smile. "The first fish in my net. How much money will he ask for his patriotism to the Fatherland? These swine of French would sell their mothers for gold." The door opened, this time to admit the old man. "Well?" snapped the Commandant.

"I have to report." Jean cleared his throat. "I have to report that six English soldiers and one officer came to me last night and asked me to hide them."

"Yes? And what did you do?" "I hid them. They cannot escape. Then I went to the police, and they told me to report to you here."

"Good. Your name?" "Jean Marie Postec."

The Commandant looked at the list in his hands and made a mark against the name; then, raising his eyes he met the pale blue ones of the old Frenchman, which were fixed upon him in an inscrutable stare. "I will send and have them arrested," he said.

"There is no need to arrest them." The old man's voice came slowly, dispassionately.

"No need to arrest them?"

"No. To make sure the enemies of France did not escape, I shot them. I shot all seven of them."

October 1942

She Wasn't a Bad Girl

by Roy Cole

"THE way you treat women is this . . ." we said. We all said it, one after the other or two or three together, and we all had something different to say. "All women are bad," said the Colonel. "The good ones are only frightened," said the Major. "I took a girl out once," said the Captain, "but nothing happened. It was a beautiful evening and we walked across the common. We just walked, you know. We held hands, but it didn't come to anything. It can't come to anything, what with a leather belt and dampish grass; beech nuts get down your neck and insects"

"Nothing at all counts," said our Lieutenant Chaffcutter with the dreamy eyes and corn coloured hair, "except the time and the place, which is another way of saying opportunity." The Padre got up and crept away.

"With all your boasting and your backchat," said Lieutenant Chaffcutter, "I think none of you have ever been unfaithful. I think not one man in fifty ever is. That's why you talk about it all the time. And the reason you don't is because you daren't. I mean you daren't cold bloodedly lay on the preliminaries; hotels, brass wedding rings, fictitious names, assignations."

"We wouldn't do anything so old-fashioned," said the Major haughtily.

"Now I," said the uxorious and faithful Lieutenant Chaffcutter, "did tread once off the path of righteousness." (the Major sidled nearer) "and it wasn't because she was a bad girl or I was a professional woman-hunter or anything. You know, as a matter of fact, that I am very, very fond of my own wife." "Ah!" we sighed softly. Because Mrs Chaffcutter was beautiful and we all loved her hopelessly.

"It was when I was looking for a billet near here," he went on. "It's a dismal business. You knock at doors and old women or maid-servants come, or old men, in tussore jackets and panamas, pop up behind a hedge and tell you their Aunt Marigold from a bombed area is coming next week and they haven't any room really, not an attic, otherwise they would be only too glad."

"We know," murmured the married ones of us, feelingly. "Nothing like living in Mess," said the Colonel, and burred with self-satisfaction into his port.

"I went down a respectable suburban street," said Lieutenant Chaffcutter, "warm and sunny, hot black shadows on the pavement. Not a sound, all the children at school, only a little cat here and there making believe he was asleep, watching me with one eye as I walked along and all curious wondering where I was going.

"I knocked at a house and a young woman came to the door. She was young and plump and ordinary. She had a plain platinum ring on her wedding finger and she looked a trifle sad with a far-away sadness in her eyes, not deep though, not really sad. 'I don't know,' she said, 'I don't know.' She leaned forward in the doorway, looking down at her feet, pondering, far away. The hall inside looked clean and bright. On the right was a lounge and in the lounge was a sofa and a big armchair which reminded me of home and made me think my feet were aching with walking on the hot pavement. 'You had better come in,' she said."

"Ah!" murmured the Major, and leaned back, sucking his lips. "The inside of that house," said Lieutenant Chaffcutter, "was warm. Warm and soft and clean smelling. I thought it would be pleasant to live there, and that my wife would get on famously with the little plump young woman: share the kitchen and cooking and tell stories to one another and go shopping.

"She said she was all alone and thinking of shutting up the house and leaving it. Her husband was in the Army, stationed up in the north somewhere, and he did not get home often. She had not seen him for fourteen weeks. She pulled a big oxeye daisy to pieces as we stood talking in the lounge. We were very polite and formal. She said, 'I will make you a cup of tea,' and I said 'Oh, please don't.' 'I was going to,' she offered, and looked me straight in the face for the first time, rather timidly but straight. They were big brown eyes and long lashes curling up like a little girl's. 'I think we might come to some arrangement,' she said, and we walked closely and in a friendly manner down the passage to put the kettle on in the little bright clean kitchen.

"'We might come to some arrangement,' she said, and cut little bits of bread and butter. Her arms were brown and soft, and I remembered how, if they had been my wife's arms, I would have kissed them and then tried to bite them."

"Ah," sighed the Major.

"In the lounge I sat on the soft armchair and watched her as she made her pretty feminine movements among the teacups. There's something provocative about a strange woman in her indoor clothes. In an afternoon frock and no hat they seem half undressed already."

"Ah." sighed the Major again.

"'I had better show you the house,' she said when we had finished tea. 'You can think about it, and I will write to my husband.' I followed her through the downstairs rooms and then up the narrow, close, warm stairs, plodding up, telling myself I was unconcerned and keeping the mad thought out of mind. I discovered another odd thing then; that you can't follow a woman upstairs innocently."

"Ha, ha, ha." roared the Captain and slapped his knee. Chaffcutter winced angrily.

"Upstairs," he said dreamily to himself, "it was like an oven. All the afternoon the sun had been streaming in through the closed windows. 'This is only a box-room,' she said. 'A spare room. I did think of letting this one. This is our room.' She had opened another door, the last, a gold and green room with a big double bed. It was a most odd feeling. It was so damned warm." said Lieutenant Chaffcutter, taking a handkerchief and mopping his brow. "I can't understand it. I looked straight into her eyes and she saw what I was trying not to think. She turned abruptly to throw the window open, but no breeze came in."

"What a nice little garden," I murmured to her politely, and went and stood behind her, close, to look through the narrow casement. I had to stand close, you see, to see over her shoulder through the narrow window.

I touched her. I put my hand on her shoulder, slid it down to her waist. I couldn't help it then, no one could, just a thin summer frock; you know what women wear in the house on a hot day. My god, it was hot."

The Major was sitting up, his eyes popping.

"She turned in my arms," said Lieutenant Chaffcutter, "and kissed me. I scarcely know what happened after that."

"I do," said the Colonel.

Lieutenant Chaffcutter paced up and down the ante-room in agitation. "She was a perfectly normal, good, loving wife, I'm sure," he said to himself. "I've never been a profligate. I had no intention. I didn't dream. It was only as I said, the opportunity; the opportunity making the sin. You'll never tell my wife, will you?"

"Never," we said enviously.

"I kissed her goodbye," he said, "and the far-away look had gone from her eye. She was gay and hummed a little song as I bade her politely goodbye on the doorstep. I have never seen her from that day to this."

We all gazed thoughtfully at the carpet. Lieutenant Chaffcutter sighed bitterly at the recollection of his sin, but we didn't mind him.

"I'd get out of this damn place for a bit," said the Major suddenly, out of his reverie, "if I could find a decent billet. You don't happen to remember . . . ?"

"No," said Lieutenant Chaffcutter emphatically, and went out to the bar.

November 1942

My Remarkable Uncle

by Stephen Leacock

The most remarkable man I have ever known in my life was my uncle, Edward Philip Leacock, known to ever so many people in Winnipeg fifty or sixty years ago as E.P. His character was so exceptional that it needs nothing but plain narration. It was so exaggerated already that you couldn't exaggerate it.

When I was a boy of six, my father brought us, a family flock, to settle on an Ontario farm. We lived in an isolation unknown, in these days of radio, anywhere in the world. We were thirty-five miles from a railway. There were no newspapers. Nobody came and went. There was nowhere to come and go. In the solitude of the dark winter nights the stillness was that of eternity.

Into this isolation there broke, two years later, my dynamic Uncle

Edward, my father's younger brother. He had just come from a year's travel around the Mediterranean. He must have been about twenty-eight, but seemed a more than adult man, bronzed and self-confident, with a square beard like a Plantagenet King. His talk was of Algiers, of the African slave market, of the Golden Horn and the Pyramids. To us it sounded like the Arabian Nights. When we asked, 'Uncle Edward, do you know the Prince of Wales?' he answered, 'Quite intimately,' with no further explanation. It was an impressive trick he had.

In that year, 1878, there was a general election in Canada. E.P. was in it up to the neck in less than no time. He picked up the history and politics of Upper Canada in a day and in a week knew everybody in the countryside. He spoke at every meeting, but his strong point was the personal contact of electioneering, of bar-room treats. This gave full scope for his marvellous talent for flattery and make believe. 'Why, let me see,' he would say to some tattered country specimen beside him, glass in hand, 'surely, if your name is Framley, you must be a relation of my dear friend General Sir Charles Framley of the Horse Artillery?' '

It goes without saying that in politics, then and always, E.P. was on the conservative, the aristocratic side, but along with that was a hail-fellow-well-met with the humblest. This was instinct. A democrat can't condescend. He's down already. But when a conservative stoops, he conquers. The election, of course, was a walkover. E.P. might have stayed to reap the fruits. But he knew better. Ontario at that day was too small a horizon. For these were the days of the hard times of Ontario farming, when mortgages fell like snowflakes, and farmers were sold up, or sold out, or went 'to the States,' or faded humbly underground.

But all the talk was of Manitoba now opening up. Nothing would do E.P. but that he and my father must go west. So we had a sale of our farm with refreshments, old-time fashion, for the buyers. The poor, lean cattle and the broken machines fetched less than the price of the whisky. But E.P. laughed it all off, quoted that the star of the Empire glittered in the west, and off to the west they went, leaving us children behind at school.

They hit Winnipeg just at the rise of the boom, and E.P. came at once into his own and rode on the crest of the wave. There is something of magic appeal in the rush and movement of a 'boom' town; a Winnipeg of the '80s, a Carson City of the '60s. Life comes to a focus; it is all here and now, all present, no past and no outside, just a clatter of hammers and saws, rounds of drinks and rolls of money. In such an atmosphere every man seems a remarkable fellow, a man of exception; individuality separates out and character blossoms like a rose.

E.P. came into his own. In less than no time he was in everything and knew everybody, conferring titles and honours up and down Portage Avenue. In six months he had a great fortune, on paper; took a trip east and brought back a charming wife from Toronto; built a large house beside the river; filled it with pictures that he said were his ancestors, and carried on in it a roaring hospitality that never stopped. His activities were wide. He was president of a bank (that never opened), head of a brewery (for brewing the Red River) and, above all, secretary-treasurer of the Winnipeg, Hudson Bay and Arctic Ocean Railway that had a charter authorising it to build a road to the Arctic Ocean, when it got ready. They had no track, but they printed stationery and passes, and in return E.P. received passes over all North America.

Naturally, E.P.'s politics remained conservative. But he pitched the note higher. Even the ancestors weren't good enough. He invented a Portuguese Dukedom (some one of our family once worked in Portugal), and he conferred it, by some kind of reversion, on my elder brother Jim who had gone to Winnipeg to work in E.P.'s office. This enabled him to say to visitors in his big house, after looking at the ancestors, in a half-whisper behind his hand, 'Strange to think that two deaths would make that boy a Portuguese Duke.' But Jim never knew which two Portuguese to kill. To aristocracy E.P. also added a touch of peculiar prestige by always being apparently just about to be called away, imperially. If someone said, 'Will you be in Winnipeg all winter, Mr Leacock?' he answered, 'It will depend a good deal on what happens in West Africa.' Just that; West Africa beat them.

Then came the crash of the Manitoba boom. Simple people, like my father, were wiped out in a day. Not so E.P. The crash just gave him a lift as the smash of a big wave lifts a strong swimmer. He just went right on. I believe that in reality he was left utterly bankrupt. But it made no difference. He used credit instead of cash. He still had his imaginary bank and his railway to the Arctic Ocean. Hospitality still roared and the tradesmen still paid for it. Anyone who called about a bill was told that E.P.'s movements were uncertain and would depend a good deal on what happened in Johannesburg. That held them another six months.

It was during this period that I used to see him when he made his periodic trips east, to impress his creditors in the west. He floated, at first very easily, on hotel credit, borrowed loans and unpaid bills. A banker, especially a country banker, was his natural mark and victim. He would tremble as E.P. came in, like a stock-dove that sees a hawk. E.P.'s method was so simple; it was like showing a farmer peas under thimbles. As he entered the banker's side-office he would say, 'I say! Do you fish? Surely that's a greenheart casting-rod on the wall?' (E.P. knew the names of everything). In a few minutes the banker, flushed and pleased, was exhibiting the rod, and showing flies in a box out of a drawer. When E.P. went out he carried a hundred dollars with him. There was no security. The transaction was all over.

The proceeding with a hotel was different. A country hotel was, of course, easy, in fact too easy. E.P. would sometimes pay such a bill in cash, just as a sportsman won't shoot a sitting partridge. But a large hotel was another thing. E.P., on leaving, that is, when all ready to leave, coat, bag and all, would call for his bill at the desk. At the sight of it he would break out into enthusiasm at the reasonableness of it. 'Just think!' he would say in his 'aside' to me, 'Compare that with the Hotel Crillon in Paris.' The hotel proprietor had no way of doing this; he just felt that he ran a cheap hotel. Then another aside, 'Do remind me to mention to Sir John how admirably we've been treated; he's coming here next week.' Sir John Macdonald was our prime minister and the hotel keeper hadn't known he was coming; and he wasn't. Then came the final touch, 'Now, let me see, seventy-six dollars . . . seventy-six. You give me - and E.P. fixed his eye firmly on the hotel man - give me twenty-four dollars, and then I can remember to send an even hundred.' The man's hand trembled. But he gave it.

This does not mean that E.P. was in any sense a crook, in any degree dishonest; His bills to him were just 'deferred pay,' like the British debts to the United States. He never did, never contemplated, a crooked deal in his life. All his grand schemes were as open as sunlight; and as empty. In all his interviews E.P. could fashion his talk to his audience. On one of his appearances I introduced him to a group of college friends, young men near to degrees, to whom degrees meant everything. In casual conversation E.P. turned to me and said, 'Oh, by the way, you'll be glad to know that I've just received my honorary degree from the Vatican—at last!' The 'at last' was a knock-out; a degree from the Pope, and overdue at that.

Of course it could not last. Gradually credit crumbles. Faith weakens. Creditors grow hard, and friends turn their faces away. Gradually E.P. sank down. The death of his wife had left him a widower, a shuffling, half-shabby figure, familiar on the street, that would have been pathetic but for his indomitable self belief, the illumination of his mind. Even at that, times grew hard with him. At length even the simple credit of the bar-rooms broke under him. I have been told by my brother Jim, the Portuguese Duke, of E.P. being put out of a Winnipeg bar by an angry bartender who at last broke the mesmerism. E.P. had brought in a little group, spread up the fingers of one hand and said, 'Mr. Leacock, five.' The bartender broke into oaths. E.P. hooked a friend by the arm. 'Come away,' he said, 'I'm afraid the poor fellow is crazy. But I hate to report him.'

Presently his power to travel came to an end. The railways found out at last that there wasn't any Arctic Ocean railway and anyway the printer wouldn't print for him. Just once again he managed to come east. It was in June 1891. I met him forging along King Street in Toronto; a trifle shabby but with a plug hat with a big band of crape round it. 'Poor Sir John,' he said, 'I felt I simply must come down for his funeral.' Then I remembered that the prime minister was dead, and realised that kindly sentiment had meant free transportation.

That was the last I ever saw of E.P. A little after that someone paid his fare back to England. He received, from some family trust, a little income of perhaps two pounds a week. On that he lived, with such dignity as might be, in a lost village in Worcestershire. He told the people of the village, so I learned later, that his stay was uncertain; it would depend a good deal on what happened in China. But nothing happened in China; there he stayed, years and years. There he might have finished out, but for a strange chance of fortune, a sort of poetic justice, that gave to E.P. an evening in the sunset.

It happened that in the part of England where our family belonged there was an ancient religious brotherhood, with a monastery and dilapidated estates that went back for centuries. E.P. descended on them, the brothers seeming to him an easy mark, as brothers indeed are. In the course of his pious 'retreat,' E.P. took a look into the brothers' finances, and his quick intelligence discovered an old claim against the British Government, large in amount and valid beyond a doubt.

In less than no time E.P. was at Westminster, representing the brothers. He knew exactly how to handle British officials; they were easier even than Ontario hotelkeepers. All that is needed is a hint of marvellous investment overseas. They never go there but they remember how they just missed Johannesburg or were just late on Persian oil. All E.P. needed was his Arctic Railway. 'When you come out, I must take you over our railway. I really think that as soon as we reach the Coppermine River we must put the shares on here; it's too big for New York.'

The brothers got a whole lot of money. In gratitude they invited E.P. to be their permanent manager. So there he was, lifted into ease and affluence. The years went easily by, among gardens, orchards and fishponds, old as the Crusades. When I was lecturing in London in 1921 he wrote to me. 'Do come down; I am too old now to travel; but any day you like I will send a chauffeur with a car and two lay-brothers to bring you down.' I thought the 'lay- brothers' a fine touch; just like E.P. I couldn't go. I never saw him again. He ended out his days at the monastery, no cable calling him to West Africa. Years ago I used to think of E.P. as a sort of humbug, a source of humour. Looking back now I realise better the unbeatable quality of his spirit, the mark, we like to think just now, of the British race. If there is a paradise, I am sure he will get in. He will say at the gate, 'Peter? Then surely you must be a relation of Lord Peter of Tichfield?' But if he fails, then, as the Spaniards say so fittingly, 'may the earth lie light upon him.'

March 1943

Art at the Hotel Splendide

by Ludwig Bemelmans

"From now on," lisped Monsieur Victor, as if he were pinning on me the Grand Cross of the Legion of Honour, "you will be a waiter." It was about a year after I had gone to work at the Splendide as Mespoulets' bus boy, and only a month or two after I had been promoted to commis. A commis feels more self-satisfied than a bus boy and has a better life all round, but to become a waiter is to make a really worthwhile progress.

After my promotion I was stationed at the far end of the room, on the 'undesirables' balcony, and my two tables were next to Mespoulets'. It rained all that first day and all the next, and there were no guests on the bad balcony. With nothing to do, Mespoulets and I stood and looked at the ceiling, talked, or sat on overturned linen baskets out in the pantry and yawned. I drew some pictures on my order pad; small sketches of a pantryman, a row of glasses, a stack of silver trays, a bus boy counting napkins. Mespoulets had a rubber band which, with two fingers of each hand, he stretched into various geometric shapes. He was impressed by my drawings.

The second night the dining room was half full, but not a single guest sat at our tables. Mespoulets pulled at my serving napkin and whispered: "If I were you, if I had your talent, that is what I would do," and then he waved his napkin toward the centre of the room. There a small group of the best guests of the Splendide sat at dinner. He waved his napkin at table eighteen, where a man was sitting with a very beautiful woman. Mespoulets explained to me that this gentleman was a famous cartoonist, that he drew pictures of a big and a little man. The big man always hit the little man on the head. In this simple fashion the creator of those two figures made a lot of money. We left our tables to go down and look at him. While I stood off to one side, Mespoulets circled around the table and cleaned the cartoonist's ashtray so that he could see whether or not the lady's jewellery was genuine. "Yes, that's what I would do if I had your talent. Why do you want to be an actor? It's almost as bad as being a waiter," he said when we returned to our station.

After the famous cartoonist got his change, Herriot stood by waiting for the tip, and Mespoulets cruised around the table. Herriot quickly snatched up the tip; both waiters examined it, and then Mespoulets climbed back to the balcony. "Magnifique," he said to me. "You are an idiot if you do not become a cartoonist. I am an old man. I have sixty years. All my children are dead, all except my daughter Melanie, and for me it is too late for anything. I will always be a waiter. But you are young, you are a boy, you have talent. We shall see what can be done with it."

"It's a very agreeable life, this cartoonist life," Mespoulets continued, stretching his rubber band. "I would never counsel you to be an actor or an artist-painter. But a cartoonist, that is different. Think what fun you can have. All you do is think of amusing things, make pictures with pen and ink, have a big man hit a little man on the head, and write a few words over it. And I know you can do this easily. You are made for it."

That afternoon, between luncheon and dinner, we went out to find a place where cartooning was taught. As we marched along Madison Avenue, Mespoulets noticed a man walking in front of us. He had flat feet and he walked painfully, like a skier going uphill. Mespoulets said "Pst," and the man turned around. They recognised each other and promptly said, "Ah, bonjour."

"You see?" Mespoulets said to me when we had turned into a side street. "A waiter. A dog. Call 'Pst,' click your tongue, snap your fingers, and they turn around even when they are out for a walk and say, 'Yes sir, no sir, bonjour Monsieurdame.' Trained poodle. For God's sake, don't stay a waiter. If you can't be a cartoonist, be a street-cleaner, a dishwasher, anything. But don't be an actor or a waiter. It's the most awful occupation in the world."

On our way back to the hotel we bought a book on cartooning, a drawing board, pens and a penholder, and several soft pencils. On the first page of the book we read that before one could cartoon or make caricatures, one must be able to draw a face; a man, a woman, from nature. That was very simple, said Mespoulets. We had lots of time and the Splendide was filled with models. Two days later he bought another book on art and we visited the Metropolitan Museum. We bought all the newspapers that had comic strips. And the next week Mespoulets looked around and everywhere among the guests he saw funny people. He continued to read to me from the book on how to become a cartoonist.

The most 'unique' faces at the Splendide belonged to Monsieur and Madame Lawrance Potter Dreyspool. Madame Dreyspool was very rich; her husband was not. He travelled with her as a sort of companion-butler, pulling her chair, helping her to get up, carrying books, flasks, dog leashes, small purchases, and opera glasses. He was also like the attendant at a sideshow, for Madame was a monstrosity and everyone stared at her. They were both very fat, but she was enormous. It was said that she got her clothes from a couturier specialising in costumes for women who were enceinte, and that to pull everything in shape and get into her dresses she had to lie down on the floor.

Monsieur and Madame Dreyspool were the terror of maitres d'hotel all over the world. Wherever they stayed, they had the table nearest the entrance to the dining room. This table was reserved for them at the Splendide in New York, at Claridge's in London, at the Ritz in Paris, and in various restaurants on the luxurious boats on which they crossed. The maitre d'hotel who took care of them was a Belgian and had come from the Hotel de Londres in Antwerp. He never took his eyes off their table and raced to it whenever Monsieur Dreyspool turned his head. Monsieur and Madame were waited upon by a patient old Italian waiter named Giuseppe. Because he never lost his temper and never made mistakes, he got all the terrible guests, most of whom paid him badly. Madame Dreyspool was not allowed any sugar. Her vegetables had to be cooked in a special fashion. A long letter of instruction about her various peculiarities hung in the offices of the chefs and maitres d'hotel of all the hotels she went to. It was mailed ahead to the various managers by Monsieur.

Mespoulets was convinced that Madame Dreyspool was the very best possible model for me to begin drawing. The book said not to be afraid. "Take a piece of paper," it said, "draw a line down the centre, divide this line, and draw another from left to right so that the paper is divided into four equal parts." I took an old menu and stood on the good balcony between a screen and a column. Monsieur and Madame were easy to draw, they hardly moved. They sat and stared; stared, ate, stared, stirred their coffee. Only their eyes moved when Giuseppe brought the cheese or the pastry tray. Quickly, shiftily, they glanced over it, as one looks at something distasteful or dubious. Always the same sideways glance at the check, at Giuseppe when he took the tip, at the Belgian maitre d'hotel, and at Monsieur Victor as they left.

I took my sketches back to Mespoulets who had been studying the book on art in the linen closet. "It shows effort and talent," he said. "It is not very good, but it is not bad. It is too stiff; looks too much like pigs, and while there is much pig at that table it is marvellously complicated pig. He considered the book a moment and then slapped it shut. "I think," he said, "I understand the gist of art without reading any more of this. Try and be free of the helping lines. Tomorrow, when they come again, think of the kidney trouble, of the thousand paté and sauces they have eaten. Imagine those knees, the knees of Madame under the table they must be so fat that faces are on each knee; two faces, one on each knee, laughing and frowning as she walks along. All that must be in the portrait. And the ankles that spill over her shoes; this must be evident in your drawing of her face."

Monsieur and Madame came again the next day, and I stood under a palm and drew them on the back of another menu. Mespoulets came and watched me, broke a roll in half, and kneaded the soft part of the bread into an eraser. "Much better," he said. "Try and try again. Don't give up. Remember the thousand fat sauces, the ankles. The eyes already are wonderful. Go ahead." He went back to his station and soon after I heard "Tsk, tsk, tsk, tsk." over my shoulder. It was the Belgian maitre d'hotel and he was terror-stricken. He took the menu out of my hand and disappeared with it.

When I came to work the next noon I was told to report to the office of Monsieur Victor. I went to Monsieur Victor's desk. Slowly, precisely, without looking up from his list of reservations, he said, "Ah, the Wunderkind." Then, in the manner in which he discharged people, he continued, "You are a talented young man. If I were you I would most certainly become an artist. I think you should give all your time to it." He looked up, lifted the top of his desk, and took out the portrait of Monsieur and Madame Lawrance Potter Dreyspool. "As your first client, I would like to order four of these from you," he said. "Nicely done, like this one, but on good paper. If possible with some colour, green and blue and purple. And don't forget Monsieur's nose, the strawberry effect, the little blue veins, or the bags under the eyes. That will be very nice. A souvenir for my colleagues in London, Paris, Nice, and one for the maitre d'hotel on the Mauretania. You can have the rest of the day to start on them."

July 1943

"*I must not smoke cigars during prayers.*
I must not smoke cigars during . . . ."

May 1947

116

Ten Months in a Strip Gang

by Margot Bennett

The Daily Mirror strip cartoons are read by more than a million people who buy the newspaper and by several million who don't. Six days a week, soldiers, officers; workers, directors; sailors, and perhaps even admirals, cry: "Let's look at your *Mirror* and see what Jane is doing." But they know before they look. Jane is stripping.

Jane and most of her strip mates are in a groove. A popular groove, or the *Mirror*, with all that war news crying to be printed, wouldn't sacrifice one of its daily eight pages to strips. Currently, the sacrifice has been increased to a little more than a page by the addition of two new strips.

Jane stands pre-eminent. She is a slender, fair girl with good chest measurements and careless, magnetic habits. In the ten months we are considering she works through two plots, both easy to grasp. In the first she is a British agent in an aircraft factory, foiling the villainous artist who steals the plans. In the second her job is to be the ersatz queen who persuades the Balkan king to make a stand for democracy. In the performance of these tasks, her legs, to a distance of at least nine inches above the knee, are shown eighty-three times. She dresses, undresses, or is undressed forcibly, to reveal the brassiere-half fourteen times; the pants-half (in pants) thirteen times, and both brassiere and pants fifty-one times.

She is also shown full-length behind some inadequate substance such as steam, nightgown, bathing costume, or towel, in twenty-four pictures. She has her clothes blown off by a bomb in four, baths in five, falls by parachute in nine, and sits up in bed in five. She has a double who is shown twice bathing, six times in brassiere and pants. There is also a girl called Gladys, who is shown wholly in underwear thirteen times and in sections three times. This makes a total of 232 exposures, partial or complete, in 260 issues of *The Daily Mirror*.

It takes ingenuity to keep these revelations from becoming monotonous. Jane climbs ladders, falls through sky-lights, runs, bends, wears fancy dress, strips for an artist, rides horses, fights, is caught in a high wind, wears dressing-gowns that flap open, and has her skirt torn off by the door of a taxi. No good pose, however, is wasted. When she is tied with strips of her own clothes to the railway line, they hold it for twelve pictures. Many of Jane's clothes are violently destroyed. In January to October of this year [1943] her losses were: two frocks, one evening dress with train, one petticoat, two pairs of pants, one brassiere, two blouses and three skirts. Allowing frocks and blouses at the lower coupon rate, this comes to sixty-four coupons. These clothes, blown off by bombs, ripped by airborne adventures, torn into strips by villains, are usually beyond any make-do-and-mend remedy.

With Belinda, the other female strip character, we move to a different world. Belinda is a gallant child, with permanent mumps as well as a curly mop. Her head is wider than her shoulders, and, taking her height as four-foot eight, some pictures show this remarkable head to be one foot two inches long and equally broad in parts; about forty inches in diameter. It is not surprising that she has a profound effect on those she meets. Her adventures are simple. She persuades a grandpapa not to fear black magic, and restores a grandson to him. She foils villains who are after a cargo of national importance. In ten months she offers nineteen pieces of good advice, is in seventeen dangerous positions, and performs twenty-eight courageous actions. Such a life naturally keeps her from school, so that she has the haziest command of English. She says "sum'pun" for something, "kin" for can. A typical sample of both language and character is: "Gee! You're not gonna punish Bert f'r telling the truth, are you, Pa?"

She is the infant wife that haunts the dreams of age; an astonishing blend of Boy Scout heroism, motherly understanding and wide-eyed, baby-faced simplicity. She says "Gee" 139 times; "Great Jehoshaphat" twenty-three; and "Gosh" fifty-two. She also says "Gulp" eleven times. She has an excuse for emotion. When she meets her Daddy Pilgrim after more than four months' separation, he at once sends her away on a barge.

Buck Ryan is one of the most lethal characters ever to appear in dramatic form. He leads a life of such violence that he was given a four months' rest in the middle of the year: the facts shown here are a summary of six months only. In that period thirteen people are killed by Buck alone, and nine by his associates or enemies. To these must be added an unspecified number shot while he defended himself to the last bullet. His manly physique is shown five times. He is knocked out twice; stripped and beaten by the Gestapo; almost killed by a bandit's knife; lassoed; and besieged by Nazis. His first adventure is a private one. It ends with the villain putting him alive into the oven of a crematorium and switching it on, happily, the wrong switch. His sang-froid is shown when he is released from the oven. Asked if he is all right, he says: "I think so, thank you. My jaw is mighty sore." His second adventure is in Corsica, where he fights the Gestapo in Ajaccio, right up to the end of October, ignorant of the fact that the Free French landed there in the middle of September. In Corsica he has fifteen narrow escapes, but destroys a seaplane base single-handed. He also learns the lingo, saying Oui for Yes. This is good enough for the natives, a typical sample of whose patois is: "Bien! Hold him until I get down and give him a frisk."

A new strip, Garth, has a hero who outdoes Ryan in sheer masculinity. However, Garth's exploits are not realistic, like Ryan's. He is the exponent of pure romance. The strip is a kind of secular *Pilgrim's Progress* crossed with *Chums*. He appears as a clean-shaven castaway on a raft, is revived by a beautiful girl called Gala, who wears a garment of bathing-costume type. The villainess wears brassiere and rudimentary pants. As these are the girls' everyday costumes they cannot be said to strip. Garth is hailed as leader, and gets involved in power politics with priests and talking animals. In fourteen weeks of this he kills a man, breaks a bull with his naked hands, moves a stone about 250 times his own size, knocks out two men simultaneously, one with each fist, and, when a rock is thrown at his head from a tower, he throws it right back up again and knocks his assailant flying. It will be realised that he needs exceptional muscles, and he has them. The calves of his legs are approximately the same size as his head, and his shoulders are three times as broad as his calves.

To round out the day's entertainment, there are three almost purely comic strips. Popeye is a big-hearted berserk sailor who spends five months in the court of an infant king, four months looking for his momma, and then concentrates, somewhat naturally, on avoiding marriage with his ill-favoured girl-friend, Olive Oyl. There are five full-length fights in this period, and 154 cries of "plop, bang, klop, bop, rip, tear, sock, crack, bonk, pop, scratch, yank, blap, wham, whop, whap, splat, whisk, clamp, snap, flap, zing, whump, thump, wump, boom, swish, zunk, dong, ding, dang, chink, clank, bing, blam, rip, jingle, jangle or skrtch," all indicating violence. Popeye is a small man. His opponents are invariably large, often so large that he has to jump, or climb on things in order to sock them at all. One was a giant octopus. To bring magic to his punch he eats spinach, "Gulp, Gulp," which acts on him as a hair tonic might have acted on Samson. Popeye has a habit of making long sea voyages in which he meets Goons, Jeeps, Sea-witches, Father Neptunes and other unlikely forms of marine life. His opponents almost always get in the first blow, and always regret having done so. The only person who ever gets the better of him is his dreamy, pedantic, hamburger-loving pal Wimpy.

Beelzebub Jones is a western sheriff; Texan in the first half of the year and rushing to help the North-West Mounted Police in the second. Forty guns, including mortars, are drawn or fired in the Texan adventure. Beelzebub acts as judge in four trials, all the accused are guilty. When western justice is done there are twenty-five villains' graves, a hat hung on each cross. On the Canadian jaunt the jokes approach surrealism. In the hair-oil country they see, under-brushes, comb trees and clipper birds. Dialect is strictly western "Yer dern tootin" always being used for "I agree."

Just Jake began again after a long absence at the end of August. Jake, a simple country fellow, has not reappeared, and at present the chief personage is a booted squire of the old Gertshire family of Reilly-ffoul. He is never seen without a broken cigar in his mouth; he buys them broken and smokes no others. He speaks almost entirely in alliteration, "Stap me soothingly, it sounds simple," and refers to his motley and bewildered household as "serfs." His life is one long attempt to raise money to prevent Arntwee Hall from being sold over his head. Experiments range from attempts to win the £100 largest-marrow competition in the Annual Gertshire show, to trying to sell the Duke of Gertshire, a notorious share-pusher, shares worth a penny at £1 a time. Just Jake is slow in action, but worked out with love. The Squire's umbrella stand is a drainpipe with M.C.U.D.C. (Much Cackling Urban District Council) on the side. The strip has a crazy, but genuine connection with the immemorial humour of the countryside.

Then there is Ruggles. Years ago, Ruggles was no more than a henpecked husband. Now he has escaped from home, with a new adventure every month. He goes to dream islands, becomes a company director, runs a musical show, and outwits Nazis with a powder that makes everyone invisible. Throughout he remains the ordinary bloke, honest, patriotic and humorous, with the same spasms of worry that afflicted him as the home-suffering little man. The Ruggles rhythm can be seen from the fact that he appears puzzled, worried or shocked eighty times, in a tough spot in twenty-six pictures, and on top of the situation in twenty-one. The most interesting facts about Ruggles are, however, that his face never changes its expression. A portion of it is sometimes enlarged, it is shown from another angle, or lines of bewilderment radiate from it. That is all. And secondly, this ordinary bloke sees the female form stripped to brassiere and pants, or less, in seventy-nine pictures in ten months. Happy ordinary bloke. Ruggles is just the man who would appreciate *The Daily Mirror* strips.

As we go to press Buck Ryan is swimming through a sewer with a bullet hole in his right heel. Jane is rushing through the streets in a transparent mackintosh, and Belinda is being received by a sinister Rajah's son at the Court of Jelhipore. Newspaper men and women sometimes flatter themselves that they get around and see things. Few of them get around as much as the heroes of *The Daily Mirror* strips, who are fortunate also in seeing things which seldom come the way of the writers in the remaining pages of the paper.

January 1944

120

The Inventions of Jules Verne

by Stephen Kernahan

Now chiefly remembered as the author of two or three dog-eared volumes in the juvenile section of public libraries, Jules Verne was in fact the creator of well over sixty scientific romances to the same pattern as the famous *Twenty Thousand Leagues Under the Sea*. In these he put forward nearly two-hundred inventions, great and small, of which over one- hundred have materialised.

His nimble mind sent travellers flying towards the moon in giant cannon balls, cleaving space at one hundred and twenty miles an hour in helicopters, and exploring the ocean bed in submarines, flying boats, amphibious tanks, chemical warfare, broadcasting, television, searchlights to project advertisements on clouds, escalator-pavements, talking films, climate-proof cities, even the modern mass-production chain-belt factory, are all to be found in his pages. For a man born in 1828, who was a lawyer, not an engineer, by profession Verne well deserves his reputation as a prince among prophets.

Often wrongly compared with Herbert Wells whose scientific novels usually deal with frank impossibilities, such as a time-machine, Verne set out, in the main, to show his world what science would actually be able to do in the years ahead. No pains were too great to ensure accuracy. He habitually employed a consulting engineer to check his calculations, and when he does go wrong it is only because he is dealing with problems of which no man in his day had had any practical experience.

Take the *Voyage To The Moon* for example; here Verne sends three men into space as the crew of an aluminium cannon ball travelling at twelve-hundred yards a second. He works out the details admirably: a cannon nine-hundred feet long and nine feet across, sunk into a hill like a cast-iron well and loaded with two-hundred tons of gun cotton, does the trick. Verne protects his adventurers from the terrific starting kick by floating their internal compartment on a water cushion. Now, so far, no human being has approached Verne's speed of twelve-hundred yards a second, though some test pilots have reached over three-hundred yards a second in terminal velocity dives. But we do know the cannon ball method is an impossibility. Verne's space ship accelerated from rest to 2,400 mph in nine-hundred feet, which would take half a second. This would subject the crew to an acceleration of over two-hundred and twenty-five times the force of gravity whereas we know from experience with catapult planes that about three and a half is as much as the body can stand when starting from rest. Water-cushion or no water-cushion; Verne's astronauts would have been reduced to a smear on the bottom of the spaceship. Yet if the acceleration can be applied more gradually, say by rockets burning in an appreciable time, the rest of Verne's calculations will still apply.

The helicopter of the *Clipper of the Clouds* was another brilliant feat of Verne's imagination. Written in 1886, seventeen years before the Wright brothers succeeded in making their first plane stay up for twelve seconds, Verne demonstrated his belief that the balloon (then the subject of great activity) would never be more than a toy, and that the future lay with the as yet unborn aeroplane, or helicopter. Robur's helicopter, the 'Albatross,' was a hundred feet long by twelve feet wide, about thirty feet longer than the fuselage of a Halifax heavy bomber. Propellers at bow and stern gave it forward motion, and vertical air-screws provided the lift. The speed of one hundred and twenty miles an hour with which Verne credited it seems moderate enough now, but it also had a three-inch cannon, a battery of searchlights and a printing press; we have only recently caught up with the first two items, a typewriter is as near the third as any plane has yet got.

The 'Albatross' was built of compressed paper, again a very shrewd shot, but otherwise it was simply a ship which had air-screws instead of sails or propellers. Verne's genius seems to have fallen flat on the details. Although he showed quite good knowledge of the behaviour of airstreams at high speed, he yet makes his helicopter quite unstreamlined, with huge flat-sided deck-houses and a forest of masts; she is quite literally a sky-ship. Her wind resistance and drag would have been fantastic; to give her the speed suggested would have taken at least eight-thousand horsepower, and this Verne cheerfully provides by special accumulators: "what were the elements and acids only Robur knew," which lasted for six months without recharging. He scores two minor bulls-eyes, however, with unbreakable glass windows for the cabins, and dehydrated foods in the cook's galley.

Still first favourite, *Twenty Thousand Leagues Under the Sea* was written by Verne in 1870. Captain Nemo's submarine far surpasses anything we have yet seen. She has a picture gallery, a library, a smoking room, a grand organ, a museum, and a separate miniature submarine for minor occasions. The details of the 'Nautilus' make an interesting comparison with the submarines actually built for the Royal Navy. She was of much the same dimensions as the class to which HMS Thetis belonged; two hundred and sixty feet long by twenty-six feet beam. But whereas in actual submarines the crew sleep in quarters fitted as best may be in the cramped space left by the machinery, Nemo's men were palatially accommodated with a kitchen nine feet long, a common room thirty-five feet in length, and this in addition to the luxurious quarters reserved for her captain.

Verne skips over the details of the engines for they are driven by electric batteries which obtain power from mercury and sea-water, and drive the propeller by a system of magnetic levers and ratchets, giving the ship a speed of fifty miles an hour. She can, if she chooses, submerge to a depth of twelve miles. Here of course Verne goes sadly astray; the fastest submarines of the British Navy can do no more than twenty-one knots on the surface, and only ten knots when submerged. Moreover, they need engines of ten-thousand horsepower to do it, and there is precious little room left for anything else.

The usual submerged speed of a submarine is a mere walking pace; full speed exhausts the accumulators in a very short time so that one can take about one hundred miles as being the maximum submerged radius of most modern submarines. But when it comes to diving, the 'Nautilus' surpasses everything with its ability to plunge twelve miles down. Unless a new record has been set up in secret during the war, we are still a long way behind Verne, for about four-hundred and twenty feet is our record. He achieved all this remarkably cheaply, too, for, minus her artistic trimmings, the 'Nautilus' cost only £137,500, as against £350,000 to £500,000 for the most common types in the Navy. For all these minor discrepancies the 'Nautilus' was a phenomenal forecast to come from the brain of a nineteenth-century lawyer.

In a later book, *Master of the World* (1904) Verne boils Nemo and Robur down into a super-colossal figure, the inventor of a combined submarine-cum-tank-cum-aeroplane, who aims at world domination and is prevented only by divinely directed lightning. Verne has another slap at would-be dictators in *The Begum Fortune* (1879), a story of the conflict between two super millionaires, one German, one French. The present interest of the story lies in his description of the city-factories owned by the rivals. The German Steeltown is divided into 24 sections, no worker does more than one job, and no worker dare enter any other section of the factory under pain of expulsion. Steeltown is busy on a stupendous cannon, to fire a huge gas shell which is to exterminate its rival, but the inventor is killed by an accidental sniff of his own poison. The French city on the other hand is much more liberal; free light, heat and telephones are provided by the authorities, chimneys exhaust their smoke into the sewers, not the air, and everything is run on approved cellophane-wrapped and germ-free principles.

Though the missionary of progress Verne could still laugh at science; read *The Purchase of the North Pole*. Here an American buys the Arctic Circle and plans to get at the huge mineral wealth of the Pole by tilting the world on its axis and bringing the Arctic into a temperate zone. Verne, as usual coolly scientific, invents the method, a monstrous cannon built in Central Africa is to be fired off, and the recoil will do the trick. The cannon is made, fired, but nothing happens, because the professor was disturbed by a telephone call during his calculations and left out a critical nought. Verne could also joke for the mere fun of it. One of his last stories was *A Day in the Life of An American journalist, 2889 A.D.*, a shrewd forecast of the American millionaire newspaper owners and their political power. In this story, written in 1904, Verne forecasts the B.B.C. and television. Newspaper subscribers no longer bother to read, if sufficiently wealthy they have combined television-telephone sets in their homes, where they see current events as they occur on a screen, and listen to the reporter's running commentary. The less wealthy patronise street-kiosks where similar sets are installed, like a call-box telephone.

After a description of New York in 2889, with skyliners landing on top of skyscrapers, with moving pavements, sky advertisements, and electric power lines and pylons studding the landscape, Verne takes us home with the millionaire to his super-luxury flat. Demonstrating its amenities, the millionaire comes to his mobile bath, presses a button and out it rolls on wheels. Out it rolls indeed, but with the millionaire's wife in it. The joke has been borrowed dozens of times by revue companies since Verne wrote it forty years ago, but probably hardly one in a thousand who sees it knows that it came from the same fertile brain as the *Clipper of the Clouds* and *Twenty Thousand Leagues Under the Sea*.

July 1944

Victorian Nightlife

by Thomas Burke

It is just midnight. The public houses are brightly lit and still open. The dance halls are still in action. Men, young and old are making for the restaurants of the Strand, Covent Garden, Leicester Square and Haymarket. Discreet gaming houses in the Piccadilly region are preparing for their nightly session. The Midnight Sons and Rollicking Rams in evening clothes are parading the streets in little bands, singing choruses and knocking people off the pavement. Regent Street, Piccadilly and the Strand are thronged with girls and women in cheap finery, walking slowly up and down. In some of the restaurants they are guests of the house and are sitting at the tables waiting for chance company. The evening of London's Bohemia is just beginning.

Is that a picture of London in the free 1920's? No; it is a picture of Bohemian London in the staid and joyless mid-Victorian years. Those who derive their ideas of the Victorian age from certain books of recent years would no doubt suffer a shock if they could slip back into that age and take a look at some of the less orderly aspects of its nightlife. They might begin to wonder whether the terms 'repressed' and ' puritanical' had not got transposed into the wrong century; whether the age of convention and conformity is not a little nearer to themselves than to grandfather and great-grandfather. They might reflect that in Victorian days the public houses were closed only five hours out of the twenty-four. They might remember that it was in the Victorian days that the music hall was born and came to maturity, that the dance hall was at its peak; and that *The Pink 'Un*'s Rabelaisian front page made its weekly appearance.

They might remember that the Empire Promenade, nightly filled with women of the town, was as much a feature of later Victorian days as Exeter Hall; and that the phrase 'Prudes on the Prowl' was not, as it sounds, a phrase of the frank and unconventional twentieth century; it was used by respectable Victorian papers against those who wished to close the Empire Promenade. Victorian nightlife, indeed, had more freedom, even licence, than anything we have known in our generation. Compared with the thin, controlled nightlife of our peacetime, with its early hours and its furtive, underground night clubs, the Victorian nights were rich and fruity carnival, open and unashamed. The young Victorian's popular anthem of refusal to go home till morning was not, as with our young men, a matter of words to a tune; it was nightly translated into public fact.

For many restaurants within half a mile of Piccadilly Circus, the after theatre hours were the time of waking up. Some of them, indeed, did not open till that time, and as they kept their own hours you had no scramble for a hasty snack before your bottle was removed and you were turned out. You could sup at your ease, and you had a wide choice of places where you could get supper and entertainment without paying ruinous prices in melancholy clubs.

One of the most popular midnight resorts with journalists, barristers, actors, and musicians was a place of which everybody has heard, Evans Supper Rooms in Covent Garden, where chops, steaks, devilled kidneys and welsh rabbits were served to an accompaniment of comic songs or madrigals from a choir of boys. Evans was a highly respectable resort. Others were not. Two of them were the Garricks Head, in Drury Lane, and the Coal Hole, off the Strand, whose entertainment was the Judge and Jury trials, bawdy travesties of divorce actions. Another, of which everybody has heard, was the Cyder Cellars in Maiden Lane, where the big event of the evening was the recital, by a comedian named Ross, of the blasphemous and hair-raising Ballad of Sam Hull.

Within the half-mile were scores of other places. If you wanted some midnight entertainment more highly spiced, there were the all-night restaurants of Haymarket, a street which, in the 'fifties, was described by moralists as "a cesspool of infamy" and "the Augean stables of London." Quarrels and fights in the streets around Haymarket were frequent, and many an innocent, after a visit to some of its resorts, came away without his pocketbook. It was at that time a street of oyster-bars, public houses and supper rooms. There were expensive places where you could get the most elaborate French cooking, ordinary English restaurants at moderate prices, down to what were called Slap-Bang dining rooms, and hawkers on the kerb selling pigs trotters, ham sandwiches and baked potatoes.

Some of the supper-rooms were just what they appeared to be. One or two were something more. They did business upstairs and before you were admitted you had to pass an inspection. The most popular and noisy of these Haymarket places, where the most questionable company gathered was, according to Edmund Yates, the Victorian journalist, the Blue Posts. And that place was kept by a quiet, elderly man and wife who, about five in the morning, could be seen trotting off in their elegant trap to their villa in Hampstead.

Cabaret in our own day has been an entertainment belonging only to smart and expensive restaurants, but in the mid-Victorian days, when it was called Song and Supper, it was provided for all classes. It flourished everywhere, not only in Central London, but in the suburbs. For modest purses Central London had the Finish, the New Crockford's, the Elysium, the Windmill Saloon, and the Adelphi Shades. Over Westminster Bridge song and supper were provided at the New Inn, the Surrey Coal Hole, and Astley's Wine and Supper Rooms, adjoining Astley's Circus. Over Waterloo Bridge was the Victoria Saloon, adjoining what is now the Old Vic Theatre and the Jim Crow. The usual dishes served at these cheaper shows were oysters, cockles, tripe and onions, sausages, welsh rabbits and stout, and the entertainment was comic songs, negro songs and sentimental ballads. Dance halls were as numerous then as now, and at all of them you could either dance or sit at a table with your drink and look on. A popular drink at all dance halls about that time was the new American drink, the sherry-cobbler, said to be very suitable refreshment for ladies.

A highly popular dancing resort was the Adelaide Gallery, later Gatti's Restaurant, and now a YMCA depot for the Forces; it had a famous band of its time, Laurent's, which came next to the band of the Great Jullien. Equally popular were the Argyll Rooms, where the Trocadero now stands, and the Holborn Casino, now the Holborn Restaurant. None of these places needed dress; they were mainly patronised by clerks, shop assistants, milliners' apprentices and young men of a better sort, "seeing life." On a more expensive, if less respectable, scale were the masked balls at the Italian Opera in Haymarket, under the Great Jullien, affairs which even the Bohemian George Augustus Sala described as scandalous in the matter of the quality of the women and their lack of costume, the amount of champagne consumed and the behaviour of the company.

Dancing in the suburbs could be had at Highbury Barn, at Hanover Hall, over Vauxhall Bridge, and at Cremorne Gardens. We of this century have seen nothing like Cremorne which was a cheaper successor to

Vauxhall Gardens. We know nothing of the Champagne Charlies and the Rackety Jacks who disturbed the Victorian nights and kept Chelsea residents awake past the small hours. Cremorne was laid out in the usual style of pleasure gardens, with a large dancing platform made of glass, numerous sideshows, and dusky arbours in which a half-crown dinner or cold supper was served. The dancing was varied by concerts, fireworks and balloon ascents.

But the general tone was altogether different from that of this century's Earl's Court or White City or Wembley. It belonged to the Victorian age, and the proceedings, therefore, were of an exuberance and uproar which public opinion of our own age would never tolerate. The evening usually ended in one or two fights among the young bloods, in which the waiters joined, in an effort to restore order; and on Derby Nights most of the fittings and furniture were smashed. Altogether the Victorians had a nightlife which, though it may sound a little barbarian to us, hardly permits us to pity them as prisoners of convention. Expression rather than repression was their note, and their young bloods had little of our own respect for the law and little consideration for other people.

According to Sala, the large provincial towns also had their night resorts and a midnight Bohemianism which went side by side with the life of the ultra-respectable bourgeoisie. The latter life is reflected in the novels of Trollope and George Eliot. The other is recorded in the memoirs of Sala, Edmund Yates, John Hollingshead, Grenville Murray, Ewing Ritchie, James Greenwood and others, and in the periodicals of the time.

Those periodicals were not all of the *Leisure Hour* and *Sunday at Home* type. Many of them were magazines that nobody in our own time would think of publishing, as you will see if you turn up an odd volume of *Town Talk, The Hawk, The Wasp, Paul Pry, The Queen's Messenger* and a few others. They made comments on the behaviour of prominent people, including the heir to the throne, which we read today with astonishment. We ask ourselves where are the Victorian prudery and humbug we have heard so much about, and we end by doubting whether they ever existed.

August 1944

Portrait of a Gossip Writer

by Don Iddon

The other week Walter Winchell, the gossip writer, whose column appears in over seven hundred newspapers, from New York to New Guinea, wrote to me and said: "Your stuff is too good for you to use my stuff; without even a line of credit. And I am such a good ally of Britain's. Hardly cricket, old chap."

At the time Winchell was engaged in a nationwide debate and row with Representative Martin Dies of Texas; he was battling radio censorship, writing six twelve-hundred word columns a week, doing a fifteen-minute Sunday broadcast, darting about the American continent raising large sums of money for war charities, answering hundreds of letters a day, assisting the United States Navy in his capacity as a Lieutenant-Commander on the Reserve List and also minding the business of a hundred and thirty million Americans.

One would have thought that this would have occupied him, or a hundred lesser men, but Winchell caught sight of an item or two in my diary which rang a bell as being his own special and exclusive information, so he sent me his rebuke; a very gentle one for him. I am not such a fool as to want to antagonise Winchell, so I wrote back, saying he was quite right it wasn't cricket, not even baseball. There has been no more trouble, and I never take, follow up, or switch any Winchell items. I daren't. The incident, if it can be called that, illustrates the "see all, hear all, miss nothing" character of Walter. I should hate him to be my enemy, and I value him as my friend.

Winchell today is, of course, far more than a mere columnist. Among other things he is the most potent individual moulder of public opinion in America. Only the President, making a big time speech, has a larger audience. Winchell calls himself a "one man newspaper." Actually he is several gigantic chains of newspapers. More people listen to his Sunday night broadcast than to any other news commentator. His sponsor is the maker of Jergen's Lotion (for smooth white hands) and he calls his quarter of an hour of snap news items, gossip, comment and solemn signing-off message, the Jergen's Journal. He receives ten thousand dollars each week for his few minutes on the air, and this, with his hundred-thousand dollar a year salary for his column, his film work, shrewd investing and syndicating, has put him in the millionaire class.

Indeed it is inaccurate to think of Winchell as a gossip writer any longer. He was a gossip writer, the best in the business. But today he is getting further and further away from items about people's private lives and concentrating more and more on the destiny of nations. Whether this is a good thing or a bad one I don't know. Winchell as a statesman is no slouch. As a hard hitting politician he is terrific. The Martin Dies I mentioned has a reputation for toughness, but he crumpled wretchedly before the machine-gun chatter of Winchell, a duel which excited and provoked all America.

What the fight was about is rather obscure. Dies is, or was, chairman of the strangely titled Committee to Investigate Un-American Activities. In some manner he annoyed Winchell and, of course, that was the end of Dies. Anyway, Winchell could never be accused of Un-Americanism. There is no fiercer patriot, more vigorous flag waver and star-and-stripes worshipper than Walter. To English eyes and ears it is all a little overdone, and some have said that Winchell is a patrioteer. Actually he is a sincere super-patriot, wired for sound, streamlined and supercharged.

Winchell's preoccupation with the waging of the war, and the making of the peace, have cut down his tours of Manhattan's night spots, but he turns up at the Stork Club at least once a week. His arrival, usually just after midnight, is impressive. The whisper goes around that Winchell is coming. There is a reverential hush, the waiters become courtiers, the customers make way respectfully, and the chief bartender says quietly and with dignity, "The King has arrived."

On the whole Winchell is a benevolent monarch. He is always being accused of having delusions of grandeur, but, as his friends point out, it is not a question of delusions; the grandeur is there. By contrast with his public appearances Winchell's domestic life is serene and beyond reproach. He is deeply devoted to his 'wife' and daughter Walda. Whether Winchell is a happy man, despite all his gaudy success, is doubtful. He is something of a hypochondriac, addicted to pills and potions. He suffers from insomnia and an anxiety complex. He never touches alcohol and is harsh to drunks. At one time he carried a revolver, sometimes two, fearing kidnapping, assault or worse.

But criticism worries him more than any physical hazard. Some time ago *The New Yorker* magazine ran a series of articles on Winchell which were sophisticated, thorough, and heavy with poison. Winchell had the Editor of *The New Yorker* barred from the Stork Club. This may not appear to the English mind as very drastic punishment, but relations between Winchell and *The New Yorker* remain strained. Strife and hot denunciation are what Winchell feeds on. He is forever battling in a whirlpool of controversy. The other week he called the august House of Representatives in Washington the House of Reprehensibles.

One thing which gets under his skin is the smear and snipe that his real name is Lipshitz. There is no proof anywhere that such is the case, and although Winchell's opponents constantly throw out the slur, they have yet to produce documentary evidence. In any event it would mean nothing if Winchell had been born Walter Lipshitz, though I have heard of more attractive by-lines. Winchell is Jewish; he was born on New York's Upper East Side to poor, but cultured, parents, who came from Central Europe. Walter had to fight hard for his present place, and he has not forgotten the wretchedness of poverty.

He became a journalist almost by accident. He started his professional career as a singer and dancer in vaudeville, but before he was twenty he was running a gossip column of sorts; a typewritten sheet which was pinned up on the notice boards of the various theatres. From this emerged, slowly and painfully, the Winchell column as we know it today, the most widely copied feature in modern journalism. It took more than five years before Winchell abandoned the life of a song-and-dance man for the city room of a New York newspaper, but he never had any doubt that he would ultimately become a successful journalist.

Once his column, lively, personalised, aggressive, near-libellous, began to appear regularly in the New York tabloids, it clicked sensationally. It was just a matter of time before the newspaper proprietor, William Randolph Hearst, lured him with a fancy salary (five hundred dollars a week to start) and soon Winchell was being syndicated all over the country. Today Hearst and Winchell often disagree, and on occasions his column suffers brutal mutilation; when this happens Walter is both grieved and wounded.

Winchell is, as he pointed out to me, "a good ally of Britain's." In fact some say he is an Anglophile. For years now he has been championing almost anything and everything British. He lambasts the isolationists and made substantial contributions to better Anglo-American relations. His dazzling success has naturally made him many enemies. The diehard, anti-everything commentator Westbrook Pegler, is probably his most formidable opponent, but in most clashes Winchell has usually come out on top, and Pegler has had to retire muttering that Winchell is a "gents room journalist." He may be that but the fact remains that on occasions the President of the United States has sent for him, which is more than has happened to Pegler.

What Winchell is after and where he is going, is not clear. He certainly does not want to be an editor, when he earns a hundred times as much as most editors put together. He does not want to own newspapers, when he already wields such control. He has no desire to enter Congress when he is already hip-deep in politics and firmly astride a bigger platform than any Representative or Senator can mount. My hunch is that he just wants to go on being Walter Winchell. And that is saying plenty.

November 1944

The Eleventh Houri

by Cecil Forester

Maybe the captain was a De Gaullist, and the ladies' husbands supported Vichy, and maybe it was the other way about. However it was, the eleven ladies found themselves the sole passengers on a little ship under the command of the captain. In the colony which they had left an agreement had been reached by which the colonial government adhered to Vichy, or maybe went over to De Gaulle. Whichever it was, one of the terms of the agreement had been that these eleven ladies were to be transferred somewhere else. So there they were, on board this little ship, under the command of a captain who was of the opposite faction.

Everything promised well, for the ship's course lay through waters so far untroubled by hostile action. Moreover, the food and the cuisine on board were far better than the ladies had had to endure for some time. They found a sheltered corner of the boat deck which would just hold their eleven deckchairs, and there they sat during the daytime, in order of precedence. At table, of course, the same precedence was observed: the wife of the Vice-Governor sat at one end, the wife of the Commissioner of Bridges and Roads at the other, and in the middle the wife of the Assistant Commissioner of Fisheries and Mines had opposite her Madame Petit, who was the only woman in the company whose husband was not a government official.

The pleasant interval of peace and freedom lasted only thirty-six hours. The second evening, at dinner, when they had finished their *blanquette de veau* and were far along with their chocolate eclairs, the captain, cap in hand, came into the dining salon. At once the chatter died away, and everyone gave him full attention, for the captain was a personable, youngish man, with a roving, humorous eye and one eyebrow permanently raised. The captain acknowledged the concentration of the general interest on him, with a little bow.

"Ladies," he said politely, "I trust you are all comfortable?" A little murmur told him that his assumption was correct. "It desolates me, then," went on the captain, "to do anything that will disturb your present tranquillity." The women looked at each other with a trace of perturbation. But the captain hastened to reassure them. "It is the merest trifle," he said, "the most inconsiderable detail, and only one of you will be inconvenienced. I am a lonely man," went on the captain. "Not since 1939, ladies, have I had the felicity of being in the bosom of my family. I yearn inexpressibly for domestic bliss. My nights are solitary, and my days are haunted by indescribable images. You will agree, ladies, that this is not a desirable nor yet a happy condition. I wish that one of you ladies would relieve it." The wife of the Vice-Governor rose in her wrath. "Sir," she said, "your suggestion is despicable. Speaking for myself, and I am quite sure I am voicing the sentiments of all these other ladies, I must request you to leave this room which you defile with your presence."

There was a murmur of agreement when she looked down the table. Yet the captain remained unabashed. "Ladies," he said, "it never occurred to me that eleven such distinguished and beautiful women could all be as heartless as you seem to be. It desolates me to make that discovery. Moreover, it desolates me for another reason. As you are doubtless aware, ladies, the captain of a ship holds certain extraordinary powers. His authority is quite unquestioned. Any passengers for whom I should find a distaste might be very uncomfortable indeed. They might be reduced to a diet of ship's biscuit and water. Instead of taking the air on the boat deck they might be confined in some compartment below the water line, where cockroaches abound, and where rats the size of fox-terriers run squealing through the darkness. It would hurt my feelings almost beyond reconstitution if I were compelled by the exigencies of my situation to condemn eleven women to such an experience." That was a gloomy picture indeed. The women looked at each other all over again, with new eyes. Finally the wife of the Vice-Governor voiced the question they all wanted asked. "What do you want us to do?" she said. "I would be grateful," replied the captain, "if you would settle the matter among yourselves. I should be very embarrassed at having to discriminate among eleven ladies who are all so charming and amiable. If one of you, in half an hour's time, were to come and seek me in my cabin, I should not merely be satisfied, I should be imparadised. Goodnight, ladies, to ten of you. Au revoir to the eleventh."

And with that he withdrew, leaving the ladies sitting over their only half-consumed chocolate eclairs. "The insolence." said the wife of the Vice-Governor. "The cruel, unspeakable arbitrariness." Then, "Please remember, Madame" said the wife of the Commissioner of Bridges and Roads, "that his power over us is unlimited."

"Rats the size of fox-terriers." wailed the wife of the Assistant Director of Posts, Telegraphs and Telephones. "Can we yield to a threat?" demanded the wife of the Vice-Governor. "Yes," said the wife of the Superintendent of Public Education, greatly daring. And as soon as she said it, it was evident that she had the sentiment of the meeting with her. "One of us must sacrifice herself for the sake of the others," said the wife of the Adviser on Native Affairs. "Then who will go to the cabin of this intolerable dictator?" asked the wife of the Vice-Governor.

That question was not so easily answered. Nobody wanted to volunteer, for fear her motives would be misconstrued. There was a silence which endured for some time before it was broken by Madame Petit, who, not being the wife of a government servant, was not so bound by convention. "Let the cards decide," she said. "Deal one card to each, and the one who holds the lowest goes."

"So be it," said the wife of the Vice-Governor, grimly. The wife of the Commissioner of Bridges and Roads rose from her chair and brought the cards from the drawer of the card table against the bulkhead. She shuffled them, and proceeded to deal a card face upward to each woman at the table. A ten, a knave, a seven. The wife of the Vice-Governor received the ace of hearts. Then the little wife of the Assistant Commissioner of Fisheries and Mines received the two of clubs, and a little sigh escaped from ten pairs of lips. "No need to deal further," said the wife of the Commissioner of Bridges and Roads. The wife of the Assistant Commissioner of Fisheries and Mines sat still, her eyes cast down to the fatal two of clubs before her, and then, without a word, she rose from her chair and ran from the room.

Next morning there were the eleven deckchairs on the boat deck. Ten of them were closely side by side, and all ten were occupied; the eleventh was empty and set a little apart, as was to be expected. The ten women were chatting pleasantly and indifferently, with only an occasional glance at the vacant chair. The wife of the Assistant Commissioner of Fisheries and Mines, when at last she appeared, slipped unobtrusively into her chair, and made no attempt to close the gap that yawned between herself and the others. At luncheon, and at dinner, everyone contrived to sit at the table with her without having to address her directly or even meet her eye.

Yet dinner did not go by without disturbance. That was more, really, than they should have expected, as they realised when the insolent captain made his appearance once more, brazen and unabashed, with the same little bow and the same eyebrow raised higher than the other. "Ladies," he said, "I hope you will forgive me for intruding upon you again. But another long, lonely night yawns before me. I feel myself compelled to ask you again to make a selection. I hasten to assure you, ladies that I have not a word to say against my charming and delightful companion of yesterday." Here the captain's eyes met those of the wife of the Assistant Commissioner of Fisheries and Mines; "but the experience was so Elysian that I am tempted to see what other blessings destiny can have in store for me. I hope that among the ten of you there will be one whose heart will be softened, because the alternative that I mentioned to you yesterday still exists, and it would irk me beyond description to have to apply it."

"You mean that you want another of us?" demanded the wife of the Vice-Governor. "Madame expresses herself with a crudeness that I should have thought alien to a lady of her breeding," said the captain, "but with perfect exactitude nevertheless." When the captain had bowed himself out, the wife of the Commissioner of Bridges and Roads broke the silence. "Well," she said, "shall I fetch the cards?" The renewed silence gave consent. Once more she dealt the cards round and this time the lowest card fell to the wife of the Superintendent of Public Education, who stoically rose from her chair and left the room without a word.

So next morning on the boat deck there were nine chairs, close side by side, and two set apart, in one of which was sitting the wife of the Assistant Commissioner of Fisheries and Mines while the other was vacant. The delightful weather and the calm sea persisted. Life was good, and nine women chatted peacefully together. Then came the wife of the

Superintendent of Public Education who arrived unobtrusively and sat down beside the wife of the Assistant Commissioner of Fisheries and Mines, well apart from the rest, whose conversation hardly wavered a moment.

Yet soon the wife of the Superintendent of Public Education stole a glance at the wife of the Assistant Commissioner of Fisheries and Mines, and received a glance in return, and it was not very long before they were positively chatting and as they chatted they hitched their chairs closer and closer together, until at last the nine beheld the outcast pair chattering away together in low tones; their heads nodding and their hands gesticulating. And every woman of the nine wondered what these two were discussing in such animated whispers. Even at meal times it was just as bad, with those two exchanging private glances across the table. They might be initiates in some very exclusive cult from the airs they put on.

So when the captain came in again the silence that acknowledged his presence had almost something of a hush of expectancy about it, and his statement that he did not want to be lonely tonight was not met by any verbal protest; and after he had gone and the lot fell upon the wife of the Deputy Governor of Prisons and Forced Labours, she rose from the table without hesitation.

Next morning on the boat deck there were eight deckchairs in one group and three in another, and immediately a most animated conversation struck up among the three. The morning after there were seven chairs in one group, and four in the other, and when the wife of the Sub-Chief of Railways arrived and was made eagerly welcome, the wife of the Vice-Governor took one look and turned away. "Disgraceful," was all she permitted herself to say.

That night it was the turn of the wife of the Assistant Director of Posts, Telegraphs and Telephones which made the balance between the haves and the have-nots very nearly even; and the next night the lot fell upon Madame Petit, and the balance was upset altogether; six eager women chatter-chatter in one group, and five glum women feeling rather out of things in the other. Next was the turn of the wife of the Junior Procureur General, and then that of the wife of the Adviser on Native Affairs, and then that of the wife of the Deputy Comptroller of Finance, so that one fine morning found the wife of the Vice-Governor and the wife of the Commissioner of Bridges and Roads left to themselves while nine eager women discussed the mysterious unknown subject.

Even then the curiosity or the aesthetic taste of the captain was not satisfied. He came in at dinner and addressed his unvarying demand to the wife of the Vice-Governor. When he had gone the wife of the Commissioner of Bridges and Roads said: "We had better simply cut the cards; low card loses, as usual."

"No," said the wife of the Vice-Governor, with unusual decision, "low card wins." If the objective of the wife of the Vice-Governor had been to ensure the preservation of her virtue one more night, she attained it, for she cut a seven against a king. Yet she stood gazing down at the seven, fingering it and turning it over and over for a long time after the wife of the Commissioner of Bridges and Roads had slipped away.

It was not long before lunch that a change came over the situation, when a long, lean, wicked destroyer hove up over the horizon with the white ensign flying astern. She exchanged a flurry of signals with the ship. The upshot was that the destroyer took the ship in to the port which lay just below the horizon. When the anchor fell the captain came on to the boat deck with his usual lifted eyebrow.

"I much regret to derange you ladies," he said, "but the British authorities insist on taking you out of my guardianship. I particularly regret it, as I did not expect any such occurrence, at least not for another day. But one cannot argue with six-inch guns. I must ask you, ladies, to pack your belongings ready to go ashore instantly."

And when the time came to say goodbye, while the boat danced at the foot of the accommodation ladder, ten women shook hands with the captain and wished him God-speed and good luck. The eleventh one was the wife of the Vice-Governor, who swept past him without a glance. Moreover, the ten had accustomed themselves to paying no attention to her, and even began to advance toward the accommodation ladder ahead of her. But with the imperious gesture of conscious virtue, she held them back. "'You are not fit to go in front of me," she said. "You are not fit to associate with me for one moment."

Abashed, they shrank back, admitting their fault. 'They were the pariahs now. The wife of the Vice-Governor sailed past them with her nose in the air, down the accommodation ladder and took her place in the boat as if she were the only woman in the world.

December 1944

Uncle Petya: Tchaikovsky's Niece Remembers

by Lesley Blanch

"Uncle Petya died when I was very young, so I don't remember him clearly. Mostly I remember the family legends about him. After he died I used to sleep in his study, at Klin, his country home near Moscow. It was left very much as it had been when he worked there: music, manuscripts, books, his piano. I was frightened of the death mask. It was Uncle Petya, and yet it was not; the bronze laurel wreath looked silly. I remember him as the moody, yet enchantingly gay uncle who made my dolls dance, who used to mimic ballerinas and opera singers or invent little tunes for me to sing."

The rest of the world remembers him as Tchaikovsky. Mrs Felix Crosse was born Tatiana Tchaikovsky; her father was the composer's younger brother Anatol, and at the time she first remembers Uncle Petya her father was Vice-Governor of Nijni-Novgorod. It's a long way from Nijni-Novgorod to the greystone bow-fronted house in Chipping Campden where she lives now.

"Uncle Petya would have liked the Cotswolds," she says. "He could have worked well here. He loved the country, the quiet. He taught himself English, you know. When he came here and was made Doctor of Music at Cambridge he was quite fluent. But he always said that the whole ceremony and wearing those robes, and the cap, made him feel deathly self-conscious, and rather foolish."

Mrs Crosse sits on an Empire sofa, an oddly incongruous figure to find in the West country. She has grown-up children, but she has that French type of chic which keeps a woman of any age from looking grandmotherly. Her hair is piled up modishly; her lacquered nails and jewellery are in startling contrast to the beige home-spuns beloved of the English country matron. She has enormous vivacity and speaks broken English with wit and ease. Her grimacing smile is mischievous, and faintly monkey-like. She settles herself in the afternoon sun, dispensing a delicate brew of China tea and doughnuts, starchily sustaining *a l'anglaise*. The room seems as alien to the Cotswolds as she herself. Gilt furniture, Empire ormolu candle-sconces, frivolous knick-knacks and painted fans.

"Home to us was Klin, the old house that Uncle Petya loved. We always spent as much time as possible there. After Uncle Petya's death my father turned part of it into a national memorial. The Soviet Government kept it as a Tchaikovsky Museum; later, I believe, it became a rest home for musicians. It was a very simple place, a sort of chalet, with wooden verandas running round. The birch forests grew to the door. We used to have meals on the veranda and the talk was about everything except music. Uncle Petya loathed talking music with amateurs."

"They used to play whist and drink tea; endless brews of tea. Strong tea was Uncle Petya's passion: he always had a samovar by him when he worked. Mushrooming was another passion; he would go for miles looking for the exact kind he preferred, or discovering the lilies of the valley that were his favourite flower. He wrote a poem on them, I remember. He used to make notes for his music as he walked. He was very methodical in the way he lived, but extravagant and casual over money. He kept no check of what he earned, spent or gave away."

"His day began at eight o'clock. He would spend the morning reading newspapers, foreign ones too, and answering the enormous number of letters which he got. He kept up with all the latest books as well. After lunch he went off for long solitary walks, carrying his music notebook with him. Tea lured him back about five, and after that he used to disappear into his study to work, wearing an old oriental dressing-gown. In the evenings he played to us. Mozart, mostly, or read Pushkin's poetry aloud. Alexander Pushkin was his god. Some of his happiest hours were spent working on his operatic version of Eugene Onegin, Pushkin's masterpiece."

Mrs. Crosse pours out some more tea and glances along the old High Street where a straggle of gipsy women are loping from door to door with their baskets and bundles. "Gipsies are gipsies, all the world over," she says. "Uncle Petya loved to listen to the traditional gipsy and folk tunes; they are threaded all through his music. He loved beggars. He never turned one away. Then there were the dogs. He loved them too. There were eight; they always accompanied him on his walks," she adds, absently tweaking the ears of Peter, her large black setter, who gazes passionately at the doughnuts. "He is named after my uncle, of course," she added and I look reverently Peter, who remains riveted to the tea-table.

She goes on to tell me how her uncle began to compose at the age of four, like Mozart, his idol. A little tinny musical-box aroused his interest first; he used to scream for it before he could speak. "Uncle Petya's vagueness verged on eccentricity," she continues, her mind reaching back into the past. "He was moody and mercurial, by turns sparkling and sulky. One day he was feverishly lively, a brilliant mimic clowning and capering around. The next, plunged in sombre silence. Any mention of his mother brought tears to his eyes. She was half French and died when he was about twelve. My father and his twin brother were the youngest; they were only two when their mother died and Uncle Petya brought them up. He was mother and father and brother to them."

"There are many legends about Uncle Petya's distrait manner. Once he was in Paris, and received a well-known French musician. The Frenchman apologised for coming a day late. 'My wife died yesterday,' he said in explanation. 'Oh Monsieur. C'est desolant,' replied my uncle, with true feeling. He repeated it. His eyes were closed, his fingers drummed on the arm of his chair. To the visitor's astonishment he began to intone the phrase in rhythm, in melody. Uncle Petya was composing. He had forgotten his bereaved visitor."

"He was not gregarious. He loathed social life, but he used to make an effort to overcome his hermit tendencies, his inborn shyness. His gratitude for the remote manner in which Madame Nadejda von Meck conducted their extraordinary relationship was one of the deepest emotions of his life. I think he suffered from an exaggerated inferiority complex. Perhaps it was made worse by some ill-adjusted aspects of his nature. Or, perhaps by the frustration of his love for the Belgian singer Desiree Artot. She was the only woman he ever loved."

"His disastrous marriage to the hysterical and uncultivated Antonina was never mentioned in the family, at least not before me, as a child. The whole horrible business, Uncle Petya's attempted suicide; that half-hearted affair of standing in the icy river to catch his death of cold; the quarrels and nerve-storms, and Antonina's madness were hushed up. There is nothing I can add to all that's been said on the subject. I was too young to analyse him. I just accepted him; he was my favourite uncle."

Mrs Crosse goes over to her writing desk and rummages among her papers. Her spiky high heels clack across the polished floor as she returns with a shabby old leather album of family photographs. I turn the yellow, ghostly pages. Blurred and faded, the Tchaikovsky family are glimpsed, far away. Snapshots of them round the dinner-table, in a comfortable bourgeois interior, plush portieres, and the family servants hovering in the background. In the garden; with the dogs; picnicking in the birch forests. There is nothing remarkable: nothing striking of Uncle Petya, either. There is a cutting from *Picture Post*, full of pictures of Klin as it was when the Germans had done with it. They destroyed it savagely. The composer's study was wrecked to gratify their vandalism. Books and music are charred cinders, furniture is smashed, the walls crumbled; havoc and desolation everywhere.

"I used to think the Germans were a musical nation," says Tchaikovsky's niece. "I thought they loved his music enough to spare Klin. Music should be international. He wrote the *Pathetique* at Klin, you know."

I ask her what truth there is in the story that he wished to end his life, and deliberately drank cholera-tainted water. "Nonsense." she says sharply, jerked from her nostalgia by irritation. "Suicide was out of the question. We were at Nijni-Novgorod. I never forget hearing the terrible, distraught cries of my father when the news of Uncle Petya's death arrived. 'Petya is dead; Petya is gone.' I remember hearing the grown-ups talk of the coincidence of his death. Cholera deaths were rare at that time, but both he and his mother died of it. I remember the spectacular funeral: the crowds: the cortege dragging along towards Alexander Nevski cemetery.

"I remember the hushed talk of suicide, the accusations against the doctors, the recriminations. He need not have died, they said, and blamed Professor Bertenson, the Court doctor who attended him. Angry mobs of students from the Conservatoire stoned the Professor's windows. Alas! It could not bring Uncle Petya back to us. But his music does. It evokes not only his personality, but all of Russia; heroic, remote, strange and emotional. Uncle Petya loved Russia with a profound love and pride. What music he would have written for his country now. What inspiration such a people would have given such man."

March 1945

The Case of the Censor's Headache

by Alfred Perles

It is not giving away any military secrets to say that there has existed since 1939, centralised in London, a Postal Censorship Department which keeps a check on all correspondence with foreign countries. Nearly everybody receiving a letter from Ireland, Spain, Switzerland or South America can tell from the envelope that the message has been opened by Examiner number so-and-so. The same procedure is of course being followed in the case of letters from this country to addresses overseas.

For this purpose the censorship department employs an impressive number of examiners, both British and foreign. Generally speaking, each examiner is concerned with one language only: his own. As a rule, the British are not great linguists. There are a few, of course, who have a thorough knowledge of French, Spanish or German, and they are used to examine correspondence in those languages. But the Postal Censorship Department would have been a pitifully inadequate service if it had not availed itself of the aliens in our midst.

The Department employs a large number of Czechs, Finns, Hungarians, Yugoslavs, Rumanians, Russians, Armenians, Arabs, Greeks, Estonians, Chinese, Hebrews, Japanese, Burmese, Tibetans, Africans and Indians. Needless to say, the loyalty to this country of all these aliens was firmly established before they were given such important and confidential jobs.

The Postal Censorship can today cope with mail in some eighty or so different languages and dialects. Every Examiner is an expert. Nearly all of them have been employed in this capacity for over five years, and during that time they have developed an almost uncanny flair; some are so good they can smell suspicion before they actually read a letter. They can tell from the handwriting, spacing, margin and colour of ink, if a letter is suspicious. Their flair borders on clairvoyance.

It goes without saying that if an Examiner conceives the least doubt, the letter is immediately handed over to a special department, where chemists, scientists and code experts, equipped with the latest devices, examine the message for secret inks and codes. Once a letter thus suspected to contain a message for the enemy reaches this department, it is extremely rare that the mystery is not cleared up.

With the exception of French, Spanish, German and Italian, all foreign languages are called 'uncommon languages.' A visit to the Uncommon Languages Department is an experience in itself. My old major once politely referred to the place as an ethnographic museum; but when I first went there myself I thought it was much more like a visit to the Zoo. What fauna. I should have paid sixpence to see some of those specimens in a sideshow. They don't talk; the room is smothered in silence. But all the strange languages they read seem to rise above the silence, forming eddies of thought, little whirlpools of conflicting etymology, which grow to an almost audible hum, if you stay long enough in the room.

One day a wholly incredible and unprecedented thing happened in the Uncommon Languages Department. A letter addressed by somebody to somebody else in a foreign country was brought in for censorship. The foreman frowned. The letter went from desk to desk, and back to the foreman: nobody could make head or tail of it. The linguists were flabbergasted. They understood many languages, but the letter was written in none of these. After a long and slightly scurrilous conference, the majority decided the letter was written in Goomba, an idiom spoken in a certain region of Central Africa. What was to be done? Was the letter to leave Censorship uncensored? The Chief of the Department gave the matter a good deal of thought, and finally decided to contact Aliens House, where they kept an efficient check on all the aliens in this country. By a stroke of luck, Aliens House was able to locate a native of that remote part of the world where the Goomba language was spoken all day long. His name was Amul, and he happened to be a waiter in Soho.

An official of the Censorship Department called on Mr Amul, and the waiter had no difficulty in translating the letter. He was paid twelve shillings and sixpence for his trouble, and both Amul and the Censorship Department were content. About a month later, another letter written in the Goomba language arrived in the Uncommon Languages Department. This time there was no excitement and no conference. The Department got in touch with the waiter at once, and again Mr Amul pocketed his fee of twelve shillings and sixpence.

But from then on, there seemed to be an unaccountable increase in the Goomba correspondence. At first there was a letter every fortnight; then they came weekly; soon there were three or four letters every week. The special department conceived certain suspicions, and a trap was set. Within less than a fortnight it was established that Mr Amul himself was the prolific Goomba correspondent. When confronted with the evidence, the waiter somewhat shamefacedly admitted the fact that he was the author of those letters. But after all, there was no law against writing letters in Goomba or was there, he argued.

There was none. The only thing Postal Censorship could do, and did, was to reduce the translation fee to half-a-crown. And Mr Amul was earnestly requested to curtail correspondence.

July 1945

The Sage of Fountain Inn

by Alexander Woollcott

Every once in a while some reporter writes a story so peculiarly satisfying to the members of his own craft that fond clippings of it moulder to powder in the admiring wallets of all the newspapermen from San Francisco to Park Row. A few years ago some anonymous neighbour of mine stuck such a clipping into an envelope and posted it to me. I don't know who did me this service, but I have mentioned him favourably in my prayers ever since. For there in print was just such a story as every reporter worth his salt has at least planned to write somewhere, somehow, some day.

It was a wedding notice. The opening paragraph lulled one with its stock phrases and complete conventionality. It merely related that the daughter of the so-and-so's had been united in holy wedlock on the preceding Wednesday to a scion of the house of Woose. I forget the actual names. So far, so good. But then the false mask slipped and the story went on as follows:

"The groom is a popular young cad who hasn't done a lick of work since he got shipped in the middle of his junior year at college. He manages to dress well and keep a supply of spending money because his dad is a soft-hearted old fool who takes up his bad cheques instead of letting him go to jail where he belongs. The bride is a skinny, fast little idiot who has been kissed and handled by every boy in town since she was twelve years old. She paints like a Sioux Indian, sucks cigarettes in secret, and drinks mean corn liquor when she is out joy-riding in her dad's car at night. She doesn't know how to cook, sew, or keep house."

"The groom wore a hired dinner suit over athletic underwear of imitation silk. His trousers were held up by pale green braces. His number-eight patent-leather shoes matched his state in tightness and harmonised nicely with the axle-grease polish of his hair. In addition he carried a pocket-knife, a bunch of keys, a dun for the ring and his usual look of imbecility."

"The bride wore some kind of white thing that left most of her legs sticking out at one end and her bony upper end sticking out at the other. The young people will make their home with the bride's parents, which means they will sponge on the old man until he dies and then she will take in washing. The happy couple anticipate a blessed event in about five months."

From the cluster of homely social items on the reverse side of the clipping, I knew it came from a small town newspaper, and from the strong whiff of corn liquor exhaled by the blushing bride, I gathered that that small town lay south of the Mason-Dixon line. At last I found it was from the *Fountain Inn Tribune*, a weekly newspaper edited in South

Carolina by one Robert Quillen. It seemed he also owned the paper.

Fountain Inn was a village of fifteen hundred people; white, black and blended, situated not far from Greenville in the uplands of South Carolina. For a time, I dreamed of waylaying Mr Quillen when, as most people do, he should pass through New York some day, but it finally dawned on me that anyone who wanted to see him would have to go, willy-nilly, to Fountain Inn. And so, in the spring, when the woodlands in Virginia and the Carolinas were lovely with the purple of the Judas tree, and the Valley of the Shenandoah was heavenly sweet with myriad apple blossoms, I drove a thousand miles to knock at Robert Quillen's front door. I had been promised a welcome. At least he had to written me that if the hired girl said "Yes, sah, he's in, but he's wuckin' an' cain't see nobody till two o'clock," I was just to push her aside and come in anyway.

On the way I made inventory of what, since first I heard tell of him, I had already learned about this Quillen. I knew that he was a Kansan in his middle forties, that the name was originally McQuillen, and that there was French and Scottish blood in the pioneer stocks that had bred him. I knew that he was the author of two far-flung syndicated features called 'Aunt Het' and 'Willie Willis' respectively, that he wrote an editorial every day for *The Washington Post*, and, most important of all, that he also wrote for syndication a batch of twenty-one paragraphs every day before lunch. These are published in some papers over his signature, and in others scattered over the editorial page and in each community ascribed, no doubt, to local authorship. Indeed, when a punditical anthologist of American humour once undertook to list the hundred best paragraphs of the year, more than half of them turned out to be Quillen's.

The income from such an output explains why he is able to sit in Fountain Inn and edit the *Tribune* for his own amusement, spurning the cure all advertisements which are the mainstay of such newspapers if they must pay their way, referring cheerfully to South Carolina as an "illiterate, barbarous and murderous" community without fear of angering the subscribers or at least indifferent to their reprisals, and occasionally letting fly with some such scourge as that wedding notice which, though the names be fictitious, is recognised as deadly truth by the crowd reading it down at the filling station, or on the steps of the general store. As a faithful subscriber, I have bitter reason to know that he will sometimes let weeks go by without writing for the *Tribune* at all. One year the subscribers found the entire issue of the New Year's Eve number blank save for this brief handset notice: "The last blankety blank *Tribune* for this blankety blank year. The linotype is busted. No can do. That explains why the *Tribune* is blank this week. It's awful, but we can't help it. Next week we'll do better. Meanwhile we wish you a Happy New Year."

And once, on Christmas Eve, in a spasm of sheer boredom, this announcement ran clear across the page: "The *Tribune* is for sale, lock, stock and barrel, subscription list, print shop equipment, paper stock and goodwill. The price is one dollar, no more, no less. This isn't a joke but it is a bargain. The first responsible man who planks down one dollar gets it. The business will be turned over to him on 1 January 1926."

More than five hundred takers appeared within a week, but the *Tribune* had not been on the street more than a minute when the furniture dealer across the way, one of the few men in Fountain Inn who had a dollar, paid it over in person and took possession. After three years of paying its losses, the new publisher found that Quillen was hankering to edit the old sheet again, so he solemnly sold it back to him, for one dollar and no other valuable consideration.

Fountain Inn is just a desolate wide place in the road. The office of the *Tribune* is a single-room shop on Main Street. A likely youngster from the town gathers the local items, runs the linotype, and addresses the issue, while another boy feeds the press and cuts the grass. The four pages are printed one a day, and the local delivery problem is considerably simplified by the fact that as each page is run off the press, the subscribers come down and get it. The telephone has been taken out because the post office is next door and too many people got into the habit of calling up and asking the editorial staff to step in and see if they had any mail.

I came to the lovely oasis of green grass, water oaks and crimson ramblers which is Quillen's own home on the highway. He was through "wuckin" when I got there, and it was he who opened the door. There is a kind of deadly and alarming quiet about him. He speaks softly. His eyes are full of sly inner amusement. He says little and his very walk is sly. He does not so much walk as glide, like a man skating on gum shoes. A tramp printer in his teens, he was spending a mean winter in the slush of western Pennsylvania when he read a notice which said that a man with a print shop in Fountain Inn wanted someone to come down and start a newspaper for him. Something in the chilled marrow of his bones bade him answer, and he got the job. It was great fun writing pieces for the only editor who would never reject them. He has remained there ever since.

When he was writing editorials for *The Baltimore Sun*, there was a strong propaganda for his moving to the Chesapeake, but he contented himself with staying in Fountain Inn and sending a South Carolina possum to the gang on the *Sun*. He shipped it in a box padded with sweet potatoes. It was delayed in transit and was, they tell me, perceptibly aromatic by the time it reached the *Sun* in Baltimore. Three days later, Quillen received this telegram: "Polecat arrived. God will punish you."

There will be those who would imply that the moment a city's population passes the one hundred-thousand mark, the inhabitants abruptly and mysteriously cease to be human beings. Quillen feels that these pretty theorists expect him to play up to them, and sometimes he will go so far as to say smugly that he likes it in Fountain Inn because he gets a better view of America when he is close to poverty and dirt and there are no high buildings to assure him that man is a wonder. On this score he has done enough lying to make him suspect, in moments of candour, that he may end up in hell. He knows that he could do his stuff on the top floor of the Empire State Building. The simple truth is that he strayed to that South Carolina village by chance and he stays there because he married a girl who would not be happy anywhere else.

I hope she continues to keep him in his place and writing pieces for its paper. In, and through him, the American stream flows on. Like Mark Twain, he could not conceivably have sprung from any other soil. He is of the salt of this land as are, in the same sense, the Vermonters I know and cherish. You may have heard of the old man to whom a pretty bird-brain from the big city once said, in the condescending manner such people always affect when talking to the yokelry, "Good morning, Uncle Bill. Is it going to stop raining?"

"Well," he replied after some reflection, "it always has."

August 1945

My Favourite Model

by Erwin Blumenfeld

Generally, I try to sneak up on reality with my photographs. My subjects are mostly women, but from time to time there are exigencies which compel my taking pictures of men. In contrast to Michael Angelo, the male torso does not inspire me. Nevertheless, my favourite model was a shrivelled, middle-aged Frenchman, with a waxed moustache, who posed for me in a red-and-white-striped bathing suit. I have no print of this sitting, but anyone interested can probably find the picture in the home of a middle-class family in the town of Sens, seventy miles south of Paris.

I was in Burgundy when the war broke out. Since I was born in Germany, my situation was very precarious. Luckily, I had just returned from New York, and still had in my possession a press card for the 1939 World's Fair. The sergeant whose business it was to decide whether I was to go to a concentration camp or into the French Army, decided I could go into the army if I could produce my birth certificate. I had to go to Paris to locate this document, but no one wanted to give me a *Laissez Passer* to make this trip possible.

The Mayor of the little town, a true figure out of Balzac, advised me to hitchhike. In fact, he stopped the first car that was headed for Paris, and told the two passengers to take me along. After we had gotten clear of the town, the two men confessed their relief that I was with them, because they had just been released from the prison at Perpignan, and the automobile in which we were travelling had been stolen by them. (All prisoners serving less than a year were freed if they volunteered for the army). It was their intention to try a little burglary during the blackout in the capital.

When we arrived it was just one week after the outbreak of the war, and the general hysteria was at a crescendo. Anyone who looked like a foreigner was ostentatiously stopped and dragged off to the police. It was not easy for me to rid myself of my two travelling companions, and it was even more difficult to get to my studio.

I finally did manage to sneak past the concierge, and dashed into my rooms like a hunted war criminal in a Grade B movie. Quickly, I locked my door, and began searching for the birth certificate. And then came a knock. I was trapped. I realised that this meant nothing less than a concentration camp. I might have jumped out of the window, but the building next door was a police station. The knock was repeated. I looked through the little peep-hole in my door, and saw a dried-up little man with a waxed moustache pressing a brief-case to his chest. I was almost offended that they had sent such a measly little person to catch me. But I opened the door and he asked very politely for Mr Erwin Blumenfeld, photographer.

His manner was so inoffensive that I was satisfied that they had sent someone from the State Department to bring me in. Before I could pursue this line of thought much further, he asked me if he could discuss a personal matter of extreme confidence. I assured him I would be proud to do all I could for La Grande Nation.

He bowed and assured me he considered me a great man. He himself was a notary from Sens. Of course, there was a war going on. On the other hand, this was his first real vacation since he had been married, twenty-four years ago. In fact, his wife had permitted him to go with a friend to Deauville. All well and good. However, last evening he had had the good fortune to fall in with an absolutely divine lady, a certain Miss Cora from the establishment known as 'The Sphinx,' who, unfortunately, was unable to leave Paris. She had convinced him to spend his vacation with her, while his friend would continue to Deauville. It would be necessary for his friend to mail some photographs of him to his wife in Sens, photographs showing him in a bathing suit on the beach, as an incontestable alibi for his presence in Deauville.

My visitor had confided his problem to a waiter at the Dome, who had recommended me as especially versed in difficult photographic problems. The price for this labour of love was no object. The moment before my visitor had knocked I had telephoned my bank, and had been told that my funds were blocked by the Government. I considered my visitor in the light of a celestial messenger who had come especially to solve all my problems. When I asked him about a bathing suit, he proudly opened his briefcase, and produced his red and white striped *piece de resistance*. I sent him to the bathroom to get himself wet. While he was sloshing himself, I prowled through the hallway and lifted the pails of sand which were meant for dousing incendiary bombs, and poured their contents on my studio floor.

With these and other means I did my best to transform the place into the beach of Normandy. My shivering skeleton of a notary, in his gay swimming suit, posed under my strongest spotlights, while a smile of yearning was draped across his wrinkled visage. Two hours later he came to pick up the prints. He was dissatisfied with them, and refused to pay until I had retouched the smile. He wanted to look more regretful, and even a little melancholy. I did what I could. I am certain that this touching beach idyll, of the shrivelled little Frenchman in his bathing suit, can still be found on the wall of the worthy notary of Sens.

August 1945

Meeting a Ghost

by Maurice Richardson

THE knowledgeable Fleet Street type, to whom we had applied, scratched his head with the stem of his pipe, and scuffed his battered suede shoes on the sawdust-strewn floor of the olde worlde tavern. "I hope, old boy," he said, "this doesn't mean that you're seriously thinking of becoming a ghost yourself?" We said that at present it was only an idea but we should like to know how to set about it. "Well, old boy," said the Fleet Street type, with a hideous guffaw, "I'd say the best method is still the jolly old gas oven."

We explained patiently that we didn't mean that kind of ghost. We meant a live ghost, a literary ghost who wrote other people's books and articles for them. How exactly did one become such a ghost? He looked at us pityingly. "One doesn't, old boy. Most people drift into it by accident, like I did. I answered an advert from an alleged literary agency and school of ghosting journalism combined, *Earn While Learning*, I learned all right. They used to send me to interview people in the news, write an article about their particular racket, and then try and persuade them to sign it."

"And did they sign?"

"Some of them. Actors and boxers were the easiest. You could generally get a heavyweight to sign anything. One or two couldn't write, so their managers signed for them. I had a lot of trouble with the brainier characters, though. The Astronomer Royal wouldn't exactly leap at the idea of putting his name to the fruits of my researches on sunspots in the *Encyclopaedia Britannica*."

"But why shouldn't he write the article himself?" we asked.

"Too busy or too cagey. You know what these academic birds are."

"So in that case you'd had it."

"Not a bit of it, old boy. That's where the agency came in. They were quite prepared to put Astronomer Royal or Rat-Catcher-in-Chief on top of my little piece, sell it, and pocket the fee, all except one guinea, which went to yours truly. If there was a stink they'd say I'd misled them and it was all a terrible misunderstanding." We remarked that if this was the agency's normal method of working, a stink must have been powerful and pretty well continuous. "You'd be surprised how often they got away with it. And when the stink became a real fume, they'd change their name and address, enrol a fresh bunch of suckers and start again."

We supposed optimistically that some forms of ghosting must be a good deal worse than others. "Nearly always a catch in it, old boy. You can never call your soul your own. One character I know, an economist and all that, acts as one-man brains trust and backroom boy to a cabinet minister. The other night he clocks out and heads for home, having written his boss a rousing broadcast to follow the nine o'clock news. He's in the snug with his feet up when they whistle him on the blower. Will he come and rewrite the entire script, cutting out all the sibilants? Seems his boss is having purgatory with his new set of snappers."

We said we didn't aspire to such exalted ghosting. Wasn't there some humbler way to start? The Fleet Street type thoughtfully polished the sides of his nose. "I did know a character who ghosted for a murderer once," he said. "He wrote poetry for him."

"Before he committed the murder, of course," we said.

"No, old boy, that's just where you're wrong. Murderer was in the condemned cell waiting to be hanged Old Happy, that's this character's name, wrote a poem, doggerel, you know, just the kind of stuff an English suburban murderer would write, and had it smuggled into the condemned cell. Murderer was delighted. Tickled his vanity no end. He copied out the poem in his own fair hand and had it smuggled back to Happy."

"But what good did that do?"

"It gave Happy's paper the scoop of a lifetime. They printed a facsimile of the poem on execution morning." We said we should like to hear some more about Happy's ghosting.

"Strange case of poetic justice, old boy. He was writing the autobiography of a Bethnal Green burglar when the Inland Revenue caught up with him and popped him into Brixton Prison for a spell. Burglar used to come and see him on visiting days and tell him further instalments."

"But how," we persisted, "does one get the job in the first place?" "Either you do it on spec, which is nearly always a mug's game, or, the most usual way, a publisher, who's signed up some promising but illiterate character hires you to do the writing for him."

"Have you ever done any of that?"

The Fleet Street type nodded. "Yes," he said. "I was in pretty low water at the time. A publisher asked me if I'd take a hundred quid to stay with an old party in Norfolk, famous sporting character, and write his reminiscences. I stayed there one summer. Grand old character. Used to shoot bumble bees with a sand gun after dinner to keep his eye in."

"What about novelists?" we asked. "Do they use ghosts nowadays?"

"Not in this country. I've heard of it being done recently in America. Bald-headed chartered accountant writes passionate sex saga; they get it signed by a six-foot glamour girl."

What about the big money you mentioned?" we asked. For a fraction of a second the Fleet Street type looked wistful.

"Never came my way, old boy," he said. "But I know two characters. One was the steady ghost for a big shot in the 'twenties. Used to pull in about twenty-five hundred smackers per book. He was also the only case I've ever known of big ghosts who have little ghosts on their backs to write for them. He used to pay a little ghost eight quid a week to help him out."

"And who was the other big money-maker?" we asked.

"Oddly enough, old boy, he's just come in. Biggest ghost in the business. I'll introduce you, if you like." We said we should like it very much, and presently found ourselves drinking pink gin with the King of Ghosts. He was a tall, loose-limbed man of about fifty, with considerable personal charm. When our Fleet Street friend raised the subject of ghosting, he at once, and with a total lack of diffidence, gave us an exposition of his art.

"I started ghosting in a big way in 1936," he said. "The first year I made over £6,000. I wrote the autobiographies of celebrities, and my agent sold the serial rights to popular Sunday papers. We used to get prices running into several thousands."

"And how much did the nominal author get?" we said.

"The subject, that's what we call them in ghost jargon, his cut depended on the price. If he was a very big name, he might take two-thirds or more."

"Did the subjects come to you?"

"Never. I picked my own. Hunted them down and signed them up; you ought to see some of the ones that got away. I've ghosted the autobiographies of two ex-Prime Ministers and one President of a European state; a young woman drug addict, film stars, opera singers, captains of industry, an ace G-man, and a Balkan king. The one I disliked least was Warner Oland, the creator of Charlie Chan. Nice chap, but a terrible drunk. They had an awful time with him on the set towards the end. Once took him thirty-five days to say one line of twelve words. Always hiding. The mysterious oriental. He was a Swede, but he'd kidded himself into believing he had a Chinese soul."

"And which one gave you the best material?" He replied: "The Balkan king. But I could only print a fraction of it."

"Could he write?" we asked.

"Never let the subject write a line. That's one of my ghosting principles. Diaries and letters come in useful. But the secret is to get your subject to talk and keep on talking."

"Do they tell the truth?" we asked.

"They never tell the truth," said the King of Ghosts with vicious emphasis. "They distort hideously. So does the ghost. He has to. He has to write about his subject as the subject likes to think of himself, and I never had a subject yet who hadn't got an ego like a barrage balloon." He smiled. "At the same time," he said, "ghosting gives you a queer sense of power."

We said that, anyway, there aren't many ways of making six thousand a year with a typewriter.

The King of Ghosts nodded. "As soon as papers go back to pre-war size and the Sundays start running serials again, I go back to ghosting. I've got my eye on a whole crop of big subjects. Feelers out already."

We diffidently and admiringly wished him good hunting.

"So now, old boy," said the knowledgeable Fleet Street type, "you know how it's done. All you need is to find a subject."

We said we thought perhaps after all we'd write our own autobiography, and ghost it ourselves.

January 1946

Wives For Sale

by George Fussell

IT is generally conceded in England that, morally, the English have always stood to the right of the line. It is equally true that the softer virtues have crept upon us slowly, like a taste for olives. We have only to go back seventy years to find the last recorded case of an Englishman putting a halter round the neck of his unwanted wife and selling her in the public market.

This unsavoury form of divorce was fairly widespread in the eighteenth and early nineteenth centuries. In 1802 a Hereford butcher sold his wife for twenty-four shillings and a bowl of punch. At another sale in the same year a wife, a child, and some furniture fetched only eleven shillings. At Sheffield in 1803 a wife was sold for a guinea. Three years later, in Knaresborough, a husband was able to make only sixpence and some tobacco. But in Hull, and also in 1806, when a man called Gorsthorpe brought his wife to market, he sold her for twenty guineas, although the crowd was so great that he was not able to complete the sale for four hours.

Sales like these were popularly supposed to be a legal form of divorce, so long as the woman wore a halter round her neck to reduce her to the same commercial status as the other animals in the market. In fact the practice was never legal, although it was always blithely ignored by the law. There is only one recorded case of an arrest being made. In 1858 a Yorkshireman was given a month's hard labour for attempting to sell his wife.

Wives were occasionally sold by a sort of poor-law conspiracy. The district workhouse masters usually made their money by contracting to maintain all the parish poor for a fixed yearly sum. In 1815 when an Effingham man called Henry Cook married a woman from another parish and then allowed her, and their child, to drift to the workhouse, the Master decided to rid himself of this new liability. He took the woman to Croydon market and sold her for a shilling to a man called John Earl, who was so poor that he had first to be supplied with the shilling. He was given a leg of mutton for his wedding breakfast, and a bill of sale, stamped with a five-shilling stamp, was made out. In the end the Effingham workhouse lost by this scandalous deal. Earl and his new wife had a large family, then Earl deserted her, and she returned with all her children to the shelter of Effingham workhouse. The parish officers appealed to the magistrates to make Cook, the original husband, support the new family, but the appeal was dismissed.

The auctioning husbands usually had their own form of auctioneer's patter. When Joseph Thompson was selling his wife in Carlisle, in 1732, he is recorded to have said: "Gentlemen, it is her wish as well as mine to part. She has been to me only a born serpent. I took her for my comfort and the good of my home; but she became my tormentor, a domestic curse, a night invasion and a daily devil." He did not get the fifty shillings he asked, but sold her for twenty shillings and a Newfoundland dog.

The husband was occasionally frustrated. There are two cases recorded in the 1830s where the wife moved to the attack and prevented the sale. In Paisley, when the wife heard of the contemplated sale she and her women friends armed themselves with pokers and tongs. The police intervened, the case came to court, and the magistrate forbade the sale. The only excuse that has ever been advanced for the sale of wives is that in the old days no form of divorce was open to poor people. But one of the least attractive features of the custom was the interest and enthusiasm of the spectators. In the early nineteenth century there was even a ballad on the theme.

The practice dropped into disuse not so much when divorce arrived, as when public opinion changed. The change occurred in some mysterious way between 1833-36. In 1832 and 1833, *The Times* gives two unemotional or even slightly humorous accounts of sales by auction. But in 1838 it reports a sale at Islington, which would have taken place at Smithfield if public opinion there had not been too refined. The woman was sold for twenty-six shillings. *The Times*, which only three years before had been treating the matter as a joke, said sternly: "Surely the police ought to have interfered to prevent such a disgusting outrage upon Society."

It took thirty years to complete the change of opinion, but in the end the practice was abandoned. British morals were back at the right of the line.

February 1946

1938

Alexander Woollcott

Alfred Perles

Antonia White

Bernard Shaw

Cecil Forester

Clarisse Meitner

WRITERS

The following writers provided essays, articles and stories for the magazine over its first ten years. Many were well-known names; others less so, while a number of continental contributors were introduced to readers for the first time.

Although reference sources have been used in the research for this book there are a few names for which no detail is available, all of whom are believed to have been staff writers using various pseudonyms. However, they are listed here as they appear in this anthology.

James Agate (1877-1947) took up journalism and was on the staff of *The Manchester Guardian* for seven years.He later became a drama critic for *The Saturday Review, The Sunday Times* and *BBC*. His nine volumes of diaries cover the British theatre of his time and he also wrote three novels and a play. He used the nom-de-plume Richard Prentis.

Robert Arthur (1909-69) became a book editor after completing his Masters degree in Journalism. He wrote numerous short stories for magazines with his books mainly concentrating on crime and mystery fiction. Arthur won a number of awards for his radio series and television adaptions. He used fifteen noms-de-plume.

Ludwig Bemelmans (1898-1962) writer, cartoonist, author and illustrator of children's books and adult novels. He wrote forty-nine books as well as an autobiography. His *Madeline* picture books ran to many reprints over a sixty year period.

Margot Bennett (1912-80) nee Mitchell, nom de plume Miller, started her career as an advertising copywriter before moving into broadcasting. Bennett wrote crime fiction for magazines with most of her eleven books being novels. In all she created fifty-three television programmes. Her husband, Richard, was an editor of *Lilliput* magazine.

Theodora Benson (1906-68) novelist, travel writer and author of twenty-six books. She was a wartime speechwriter for the Ministry of Information. A number of her magazine short stories were written jointly with Betty Askwith.

Lajos Biro (1880-1948) real surname Blau, was a novelist, playwright and screenwriter who wrote the scripts for thirty-nine films. He worked as a scenario chief for London Film Productions under the direction of Alexander Korda.

Don Iddon

Ernest Hemingway

Erwin Blumenfeld

Ferenc Molnar

George Lansbury

Gerald Tyrwhitt-Wilson

Lesley Blanch (1904-2007) studied at the Slade School of Fine Art moving on to be a scenery designer and book illustrator. She subsequently became a writer, historian and traveller with many of her fifteen books being about Middle East people, customs and culture.

Erwin Blumenfeld (1897-1969) one of the best photographers of the twentieth-century. Working for *Harper's Bazaar, Vogue* and *Life* magazines his fashion work was in constant demand. He wrote poetry and occasional articles with his autobiography being reprinted a number of times.

John Brophy (1899-1965) teacher, journalist and author who had over forty books published. After leaving the teaching profession he became an advertising copywriter before writing full-time. His novels mainly reflected his time in the military. He became a drama critic for *The Daily Telegraph, Time and Tide* and the *BBC*, as well as editing *John O'London's Weekly*.

Thomas Burke (1886-1945) novelist, journalist and poet had his first article published, when aged fourteen, in the magazine *Spare Moments*. He subsequently wrote in *The English Review, The New Witness* and *Colour* about immigrants in east London. Some of his stories were used in the film industry. His autobiography was said to be fictional.

Karel Capek (1890-1938) writer, playwright, critic and journalist. He became best known for his science fiction novels and for introducing the word 'robot.' He spent most of the inter-war years working for *Lidove Noviny* [The People's Newspaper] in Prague. He was nominated seven times for the Nobel Prize in Literature.

Henry Cecil (1902-76; real surname Leon; other nom-de-plume Clifford Maxwell) barrister, judge and writer. He wrote twenty-five novels mainly about the legal system, two of which became films. Cecil contributed stories to a number of magazines as well as seven books of non-fiction.

Sidonie-Gabrielle Colette (1873-1954) known generally by her surname, was an author, mime, actress, screenwriter and journalist. She wrote thirty-one novels of which twenty-six were made into films. A further five films and some twenty biographies were made about her life.

Rosita Forbes (1890-1967; born Joan Torr) travel writer, author, explorer, screenwriter, lecturer and novelist. Wrote eighteen books about her travels, mainly concentrating on North Africa, as well as a number of novels.

Cecil Forester (1899-1966; real name Cecil Louis Troughton-Smith) novelist, film adapter and magazine writer. Had forty-four novels published

Henry Cecil

Irene Morris

James Agate

John Brophy

Karel Capek

Karl Larsen

most of which were about naval warfare; eighteen of non-fiction and contributed to a dozen films. He spent six years with the Ministry of Information.

George Fussell (1889-1990) an agricultural historian who wrote over twenty books and in excess of six-hundred articles on the topic. He was published in *The Journal of the Ministry of Agriculture* and *Agricultural History*. He founded *The British Agricultural History Society* and assisted in the creation of equivalent Societies in America and Germany.

Leslie Halward (1905-76) author, magazine writer, radio playwright and broadcaster. Contributed to numerous periodicals with his *BBC* dramas and plays reflecting working-class life between the wars.

Ernest Hemingway (1899-1961) an American novelist, short-story writer, author and journalist. Started on *The Kansas City Star*, then *The Toronto Star*. His novels have become scholarly classics and he won a Pulitzer Prize for Fiction (1953) and was awarded the Nobel Prize in Literature (1954).

Kathleen Hewitt (1893-1980; nom-de-plume Dorothea Martin) author, book editor, magazine writer and playwright. She wrote twenty-four mystery and thriller novels

Donald Iddon (1913-79) for many years ran the Associated Newspapers' New York Bureau. He had been a journalist with *The Sunday Dispatch* and on his move to America also contributed to a number of magazines. His books were mainly anthologies of his columns.

Sydney Jacobson (1908-88) after leaving university he joined the editorial staff of *The Statesman* newspaper in Calcutta. On his return to London he became Assistant Editor of *Lilliput*, then a sub-editor on *Picture Post*. He moved on to edit *Leader* magazine after which he was appointed as political editor of the *Daily Mirror*. He edited *The Daily Herald* before being created a Life Peer in 1975.

Stephen Kernahan (1908-80) was the son of prolific authors and he, in turn, became a short-story writer and magazine editor. He succeeded his father as literary adviser to publishers *Ward, Lock & Co.*

Odette Keun (1888-1978) socialist, writer, journalist and author who travelled widely and wrote extensively about her experiences. She had many lovers, writing a book about her time with each one. Her thirty published titles have had many reprints.

Kathleen Hewitt

Lajos Biro

Lesley Blanch

Leslie Halward

Ludwig Bemelmans

Margot Bennett

George Lansbury (1859-1940) politician, editor, author and social reformer. He helped to establish *The Daily Herald* becoming its first editor. For two years he held a post in the Cabinet, becoming Leader of the Labour Party in 1932. In all he wrote twelve books but also contributed numerous articles to various newspapers and magazines.

Karl Larsen (1860-1931) was an expert on Scandinavian folklore and able to write and speak many dialects and languages. He wrote on the subject worldwide for both magazines and newspapers.

Stephen Leacock (1869-1944) academic, teacher, political scientist, writer, broadcaster, humorist and author. His prodigious output included over one-hundred and fifty magazine articles; thirty books of humour; twenty-three works on economics and many academic papers. He has been the subject of two biographies.

Clarisse Meitner (1891-1959) an Austrian journalist, translator and writer. Her popular short stories were published in many Continental newspapers and magazines although only a few in Britain.

Ferenc Molnar (1878-1952; real surname Neumann) was a Hungarian born writer, stage director, novelist, dramatist, playwright and poet. He wrote sixteen plays and six books most of which were considered literary works of art.

Irene Morris (1920-2021) was a short-story writer whose main body of magazine work was published during the war. Her husband, Eric Mutton, was an author whose work she edited.

Alfred Perles (1897-1990) started as a journalist in the Paris office of *The Chicago Tribune* before becoming co-publisher of a French magazine *The Booster*. He then produced a number of books some of which were about his life-long friendship with the American writer Henry Miller. He was known latterly as Alfred Barret.

John Peskett (1906-91; first name Sidney) spent most of his career at the *BBC* where he was a broadcaster. He contributed short-stories to magazines and wrote eleven books of fiction.

Victor Pritchett (1900-97) writer, broadcaster, author, academic, literary critic and lecturer. He was known particularly for his short stories many of which were collated into volumes. His non-fiction works were on literary biography and criticism.

Odette Keun

Rhoda Somervell

Robert Arthur

Rosita Forbes

Sidonie-Gabrielle Colette

Stephen Leacock

Maurice Richardson (1907-78) studied at Oxford and moved into a career in journalism. He contributed to *Left Review* and *Lilliput* where he wrote under the name of Charles Raven. Later he became a book reviewer, then *The Observer*'s television critic and a sports journalist on *The Guardian*. He had over thirty books published.

Bernard Shaw (1856-1950) playwright, critic, author, novelist, writer, dramatist, political activist. His influence on the theatre, culture and politics lasted to his death and beyond. He was awarded the Nobel Prize in Literature (1925).

Rhoda Somervell (1898-1948; nee Boddam, aka Marie Troubetzkoy, nom-de-plume Gay Desmond) writer, author, socialite, actress, novelist. Most of her books were published in France due to British censorship. Her early death was considered suspicious.

Edward Stevenson (1896-1987) studied at the Art Students League of New York; landscape painter, writer, illustrator, comic-book artist.

Gerald Tyrwhitt-Wilson (1883-1950) magazine writer, composer, novelist, painter, author. Wilson succeeded to the peerage in 1918, becoming Lord Berners. He was a talented musician, skilled artist and proficient writer having nine books published as well as many articles.

Antonia White (1899-1980; born Eirene Botting) was an author, actress, translator and writer. She wrote twelve novels and translated eighteen books into English. She was a copywriter in an advertising agency for some years; worked for the *BBC*, and contributed to a number of magazines.

Alexander Woollcott (1887-1943) an American drama critic, actor, playwright, broadcaster, essayist, editor and raconteur. He was a commentator for *The New Yorker* magazine; contributed columns to *The New York Times* and gave talks on *CBS Radio*.

Other Writers

Cole, Roy
Corvin, Michael (nom-de-plume of Leo Freund)
Curtis, Douglas
Darwall, Richard (staff writer)
Graham, Michael (1898-1972)
Howard, Stanley
Makepeace, James
Sagunt, Carl

Theodora Benson

Thomas Burke

Victor Pritchett

David Langdon

Peter Arno

Ronald Searle

Conversation Piece

MRS. HENDERSON wore the old medallion around her neck with an abiding pride. She bought it some years ago in China and it was always a conversation piece when friends gathered and duly admired the bizarre piece of art. She became so fond of it that she adopted it as her good luck charm.

On a trip to Washington she met the Chinese ambassador, who studied the medallion with the faint trace of a smile. "You've seen one of these before, Ambassador?" she inquired.

He said he had, then proceeded to change the subject. Mrs. Henderson went back to the medallion. "Ambassador," she asked, "would you be good enough to translate the inscription on it?" He said he would rather not, but Mrs. Henderson insisted.

"Very well, Madam," he sighed. "It says, 'Licensed Prostitute, City of Shanghai'."

May 1943

Lilliput Magazine

A History and Bibliography

Chris Harte

SHP

Copies Available From Dodman Books

.